Astoria

An Oregon History

by Karen L. Leedom

Rivertide Publishing
www.rivertidepublishing.com

Published by: Rivertide Publishing
                www.rivertidepublishing.com

Unless otherwise credited, all photos are from the author's personal collection.
Photo on title page: *Astoria from Uppertown, looking out the mouth of the Columbia River*, circa 1912. Library of Congress PAN US GEOG-Oregon no. 39.
Front cover painting by Bill W. Dodge, courtesy of the artist.
Back cover photo of Native Americans in 1911 courtesy Library of Congress (see pages 112-113 for full image and attribution).

ISBN 978-0-87071-166-4

Library of Congress Control Number: 2010902313

9 8 7 6 5 4

Printed in the United States of America

Distributed by Oregon State University Press

C O N T E N T S

Introduction 1

1: Early Exploration 1500-1806 3
   Maritime Exploration 4
   The Mighty Columbia 8
   The Chinookan People 10
   Lewis and Clark 14

2: The Fur Trade 1806-1840 19
   Establishing a Northwest Fur Trade 20
   The *Tonquin* Disaster 22
   Trading Post Becomes a Fort 22
   War of 1812 24
   Treaty of Ghent 26
   Hudson's Bay Company 27
   Disease Takes a Toll 28
   Chief Comcomly's Head 29
   Ranald MacDonald 30

3: Early Astoria 1840-1860 33
   Westward Migration 34
   Settling in Astoria 34
   Export Economy 38
   A Town Divided 42
   Delivering the Mail 46
   River Transportation 48
   Maritime Safety 52
   Losing Their Land 56
   A Town Slowly Emerges 58

4: Boom Times 1860-1900 61
   Homesteading 62
   Preparing for Defense 62
   The Big Cheese 63
   Fishing the Columbia 64
   Columbia River Canneries 68
   Chinese Cannery Workers 70
   Newspaper Man 75
   On the Wild Side 78
   Shanghaied 80
   Fire of 1883 82
   Getting Around 84
   Astoria's Churches 85
   Building the South Jetty 88
   Columbia River Lights 90
   Early Coast Guard 92

The Railroad 93
Improved Logging 95
Ellis Island of the Columbia 97
The Strike of 1896 100
Woman Surgeon 102
Prohibition 104
Women's Rights 106

5: Hopes and Shattered Dreams 1900-1922 .... **109**
Still Growing 110
The Centennial Year 110
Socialism in Astoria 113
Modern Transportation 116
Declining Salmon 118
Logging 118
First World War 120
Ku Klux Klan 121
Fire of 1922 124

6: Rising from the Ashes 1922-1950 .... **129**
Rebuilding 130
Astoria Column 131
Swimming the Columbia 133
The Great Depression 136
Second World War 137
Cable TV 141

7: Modern Times 1950-Present Day **143**
Falling Asleep 144
Where Are They Now? 144
Modern Coast Guard 146
Navigating the River 148
Bridge to Nowhere 150
Hurray for Hollywood 151
A Bright Red Trolley 154
A New Awakening 154

8: Self-Guided Tour: Astoria Area **163**

9: Self-Guided Tour: Along the River **173**

10: Self-Guided Tour: Downtown Astoria **179**

11: Chronology **187**
Endnotes 197
Bibliography 203
Acknowledgments 209
Author 211
Index 213

DEDICATION

Dedicated to the people of Astoria: past, present, and future.

CROSSING THE BAR

Sunset and evening star,

And one clear call for me!

And may there be no moaning of the bar,

When I put out to sea.

But such a tide as moving seems asleep,

Too full for sound or foam,

When that which drew from out the boundless deep

Turns again home.

Twilight and evening bell,

And after that the dark!

And may there be no sadness of farewell,

When I embark.

For though from out our bourne of Time and Place

The flood may bear me far,

I hope to see my Pilot face to face,

When I have crossed the bar.

Alfred, Lord Tennyson

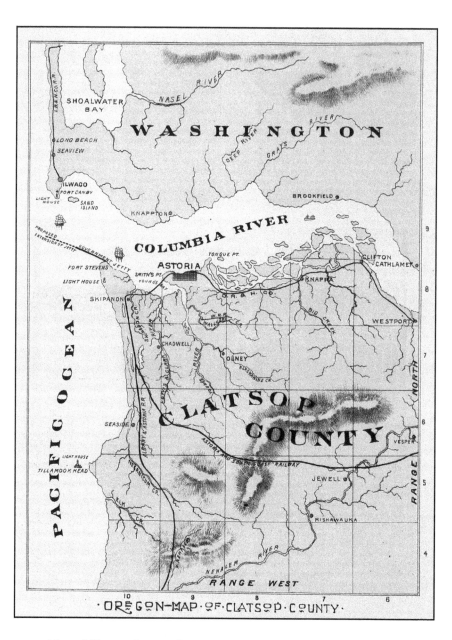

Map of Clatsop County, Oregon, circa post-1880s. Courtesy Library of Congress, General Collections Division, [F884.A8.A85].

INTRODUCTION

Astoria today. Courtesy Larry Kellis Photography.

The rest of the country is just beginning to discover the marvels of our gem at the mouth of the Columbia River—the area the Clatsop and Chinook people called home for thousands of years, where the Lewis and Clark expedition spent a wet, miserable winter, where John Jacob Astor hoped to make a fortune in the fur trade, and where the salmon capital of the world once resided.

Founded in 1811, Astoria is the oldest European American settlement west of the Rockies. It is often referred to as "little San Francisco" because of the abundant Victorian homes that cling to the steep streets overlooking the harbor, many of them listed on the National Register of Historic Homes.

Few had even heard of Astoria, Oregon, until the Lewis & Clark Bicentennial generated a nationwide interest in Oregon's scenic north coast. Today, hardly a day goes by that a gaggle of tourists isn't seen parading through Astoria's streets. Major cruise lines regularly call on

1

Astoria, and stern wheelers and other boats pause on their way up and down the Columbia.

This history of Astoria was written to offer the reader a glimpse into Astoria's vast and colorful past, providing a chronological trip through the ages, from the early explorers in their primitive sailing vessels to present day sightseers on their cruise ships.

Numerous descendants of the immigrants who settled in Astoria still live in the area. This history focuses primarily on that ancestry.

A chronology of events from the 1500s to present day can be found in the appendix, along with self-guided tours of downtown and the riverfront, and a listing of things to do and places to visit in the Astoria area.

Whether you're a born and bred Astorian, or just passing through, Astoria's history is rife with drama that will captivate and inspire you. So settle into a comfortable chair and enjoy this journey through time.

Early Exploration
1500-1806

The Columbia Rediviva, *under the command of Captain Robert Gray, was the first recorded ship to enter the Columbia River. Courtesy Library of Congress, General Collections Division, [F881.078].*

Maritime Exploration

It is hard to picture what the area we now call Astoria looked like several hundred years ago. It is equally difficult to imagine the hardships the early European explorers endured during their long voyages at sea. A passage from the east coast of North America to the Pacific Northwest might take a year or more to complete and was fraught with danger—menacing seas and likely encounters with hostile natives or other sailing ships were a constant worry. Sailors often went months without eating fresh fruits or vegetables, resulting in a debilitating condition known as scurvy.

Exploration along the west coast of the North American continent began about five hundred years ago with the Spanish. After successfully invading Mexico and South America, and amassing a wealth of precious metals and jewels from both the Aztec and Incan civilizations, the Spanish were greedy for more. They imagined northern Indians with caches of gold, silver and precious jewels. They also heard rumor of a possible Northwest Passage across the continent that would connect the Pacific and Atlantic oceans. The first person to claim to have discovered this passage was Spanish explorer Juan de Fuca in 1592. But what he discovered is the area now known as Puget Sound off the coast of Washington.

By 1600, European monarchs began to exert their authority over larger territories, and British and French seamen joined the Spanish along the west coast of the North American continent. Maritime activity in the Pacific Northwest further increased in the late 1700s with the burgeoning fur trade.

Russia's severe winter weather created a large demand for furs, so in 1766, Catherine the Great began a fur trading operation in the newly discovered territory of Alaska. The Spanish, meanwhile, fearing the Russians would move southward and establish trading posts or military bases, sent ships to spy on them.

In 1775, Bruno de Heceta commanded one of these Spanish spying expeditions. After landing his ship *Santiago* on the coast of Washington and claiming the Pacific Northwest for Spain, Heceta was sailing home to Mexico when he sighted a large turbulent bay between two capes. Heceta named it Rio San Rogue. Unfortunately for Heceta, his crew was beset with scurvy and in no condition to navigate the powerful currents. Heceta did manage to map the area before continuing on his way, barely making it home. His maps and detailed description of the currents are evidence that he was, in fact, at the mouth of what we now call the Columbia River.

For decades the British searched unsuccessfully along the eastern North American coast for an easier sailing route to the Orient. In 1776, England's King George III determined to find out once and for all if such a passage existed. He hired Captain James Cook, an experienced and accomplished seaman, to lead an expedition to the Pacific Northwest.

Cook's ships rounded Cape Horn and sailed up the Pacific Coast, reaching the west coast of North America in February 1778. Cook missed both the Columbia River and Puget Sound because of bad weather. Seeking a sheltered bay in which to repair his ships, Cook sailed into Nootka Sound, a Spanish settlement on the west coast of Vancouver Island, an area that would become the center of the Pacific Coast fur trade. Once repairs were made, Cook navigated north, charting the rugged coastline and eventually making his way into the Bering Sea. His ships passed through the Arctic Ocean, but blocked by ice, could go no further. Concluding that a Northwest Passage did not exist, Cook turned his thoughts to commerce after meeting a successful fur trader.

Spain and Russia had been able to keep their fur trading a secret from the rest of the world until Cook's men returned to Great Britain. (Cook was killed in the Sandwich Islands, now called Hawaii, in February 1779.) Once they were back in England, news spread quickly of Cook's discovery of furs in the Pacific Northwest and the high prices paid for sea otter pelts in the Far East. The reports generated excitement among fur traders, and Cook's detailed maps and observations helped open up the Pacific Coast to further exploration and trade.

When word arrived in Boston that sea otter pelts could be sold for great profits in China, Joseph Barrell & Company purchased and reconditioned two vessels, acquired equipment for a three-year voyage, and loaded their ships with goods they thought would be prized by the northwest tribes—beads, buttons, blankets, calico, knives, and other trinkets—merchandise to be traded for the coveted pelts.

The company hired Captain John Kendrick, age forty-seven, to lead this first American trading expedition to the North Pacific. He took command of the eighty-three-foot *Columbia Rediviva*. Captain

Robert Gray, thirty-two years old at the time, was placed in charge of the smaller sloop *Lady Washington*. Both men were experienced sea captains and had served in the navy during the American Revolution. The combined crews of both ships numbered about fifty men.

In October 1787, the two vessels departed Boston harbor for the unknown. The voyage was to be a long one, rounding Cape Horn to the northern Pacific where they would trade their goods for furs, and then on to China where they hoped to garner great profits before returning home to Boston. Upon reaching Cape Horn the ships encountered rough and stormy seas and they lost sight of each other. Kendrick and Gray reportedly did not get along, so Gray was not disappointed to leave the *Columbia* behind. Gray continued alone, landing about ten months later near present-day Garibaldi on the Oregon Coast. Gray and his crew initially found the coastal tribes friendly, but a misunderstanding resulted in a confrontation and the death of a cabin boy. Gray quickly fled, naming the place "Murderers' Harbour."

Almost a year after leaving Boston, Gray and the *Lady Washington* sailed into Nootka Sound on Vancouver Island. A week later, Captain Gray spotted a sail on the horizon belonging to the long lost *Columbia*. Gray and Kendrick remained on Vancouver Island for the winter, making needed repairs to their ships, and amassing a large number of sea otter skins. Then, for reasons unknown, Kendrick stayed behind with the *Lady Washington* and ordered Gray to transport the furs to China in the *Columbia Rediviva*.

Captain Gray completed the voyage, returning to Boston in August 1790, becoming the first American to circumnavigate the globe. At the time, George Washington was president and Thomas Jefferson was secretary of state. But Gray wasn't given much time to savor his accomplishment. Six weeks later, the *Columbia* was refitted and Gray again set sail for the Pacific Northwest.

Gray intended to return to Vancouver Island, where he knew furs were plentiful. Traveling north along the Pacific coastline, he spotted what appeared to be the mouth of a large river, but violent waves kept him from investigating. Instead, Gray continued north and sailed throughout Puget Sound. Then, needing to assuage his curiosity, he turned his ship around and make a second attempt at entering the river.

Along the way he met the British naval ship, *Discovery*, commanded by Captain George Vancouver—the British were still searching for the elusive Northwest Passage. The captains exchanged greetings and Gray told Vancouver about his foiled attempts to enter what he thought was a large river. Vancouver had also noted signs of an outward flow, but considered it to be insignificant, relying instead on previous reports of fellow Englishman Captain John Meares.

Captain Meares in 1788 had explored the same area using Heceta's earlier charts, but doubted the reports of the Spanish and concluded that a river did not exist. Meares gave Cape Disappointment its name, not realizing that the cape was in fact the north entrance to an enormous river. As for Captain Vancouver, he noted in his journal: "If any river should be found, it must be a very intricate one and inaccessible to vessels of our burden." (1)

Within two weeks of his meeting with Vancouver, Captain Robert Gray approached the river entrance in favorable weather and was able to cross the sandbar. He wrote in his log on May 11, 1792:

When we were over the bar, we found this to be a large river of fresh water, up which we steered. Many canoes came along side. At 1:00 p.m., came to with a small bower, in ten fathoms, black and white sand. The entrance between the bars bore west-south-west, distant ten miles; the north side of the river a half mile distant from the ship; the south side of the same two and a half miles' distance; a village on the north side of the river west by north, distant three quarters of a mile. Vast numbers of natives came alongside; people employed in pumping the salt water out of our water casks, in order to fill with fresh, while the ship floated in. So ends. (2)

The Chinookan people greeted Gray and his crew amiably, and a spirited exchange of goods left Gray with several hundred beaver and sea otter pelts. Captain Gray named the river Columbia, for his ship, and spent the next ten days exploring its lower regions. He named the cape to the south Adam's Point, for the vice president of the United States, and the cape to the north Cape Hancock, for the governor of Massachusetts (although Cape Disappointment is the name that stuck). Although Gray made no formal declaration of possession, his actions gave the United States its first claim to the Oregon Country and established U.S. presence for the first time in Western America.

Gray returned to Vancouver Island, leaving a chart showing the river's location. At the time of Gray's return, Captain Kendrick was trading furs in China. Captain Vancouver on the other hand, was most likely astounded to learn of Gray's discovery. After studying Gray's charts, he hastily dispatched his second in command to investigate the river. Lieutenant William Broughton explored the newly-found Columbia River in the *Chatham*, sailing as far as present-day Vancouver, Washington, charting and naming features along the way. He named Young's River after Sir George Young of the British Royal Navy. Years later, the name was given to the bay as well. Broughton convinced himself that Gray had not actually entered the Columbia River, and he proceeded, unsuccessfully, to claim the river and its territory for England.

Captain Gray's discovery apparently was not noteworthy at the time, because he returned to Boston without fanfare or celebration. Gray received no recognition or wealth during his lifetime, dying in poverty in 1806. Captain Kendrick, having commandeered the *Lady Washington*, continued in the fur trade business, keeping all profits to himself until his death in December 1794. While in a Honolulu harbor, a British sailing ship firing a salute accidentally struck the *Lady Washington*, killing Captain Kendrick as he sat at his table on the deck.

The Mighty Columbia

The river that remained undetected to Europeans for centuries is the largest river flowing into the Pacific Ocean along the coasts of North and South America. Beginning its twelve hundred-mile journey in British Columbia, Canada, this mighty river emerges from Columbia Lake, between the Rocky Mountains to the east and the Purcell Mountains to the west. It initially flows northwestward before heading south through Washington where it is joined by the Snake River. The Columbia then turns westward, forming the border between Washington and Oregon.

For millions of years, its rushing waters have worn away the mountains, turning the rock into sand. The Columbia collects this sediment as it twists and turns its way to the sea, and when the river finally crashes headlong into the incoming waves, it surrenders its cargo. Gathering up much of the sand, the ocean then deposits it on the beaches of Oregon and southern Washington. The sand remaining at the mouth of the river is called "the bar."

An average of 150 billion gallons of fresh water spills daily into the Pacific Ocean, with plumes of fresh water sometimes stretching as far

*Chinook burial canoe, dedicated April 12, 1961
at Astoria's 150th anniversary.*

south as San Francisco and as far north as the Strait of Juan de Fuca. The incoming tide collides with the turbulent river with a force that has been compared to the collision of two freight trains—a perilous combination resulting in extremely rough seas, especially where the sand collects at the Columbia River bar. Often referred to as the "Graveyard of the Pacific," this part of the river is responsible for the demise of almost two thousand vessels and is especially treacherous during winter storms when wind-driven swells often reach twenty to thirty feet.

Ships in the early days were quite small and of light draft compared with the large ships of today. Captain Gray's *Columbia Rediviva*, for example, had almost the same dimensions as today's bar pilot boat *Columbia*, which is eighty-two feet long with a beam of 23.5 feet. With rudimentary charts (or, in the earliest days, no charts) to guide them, and with weather forecasting limited to the "glass" (barometer) or the seaman's eye, it is no wonder there were so many shipwrecks.

Lieutenant Charles Wilkes of the U.S. Navy commanded the first United States exploring expedition to the Pacific Ocean in 1838. When Wilkes encountered the violent entrance to the Columbia River, he described it as "one of the most feared sights that can possibly meet the eye of the sailor." (3) Wilkes' survey of the river in 1841 showed that sands near the river's mouth continually shifted, changing the depths at the river's entrance, which made it extremely difficult to create accurate navigation charts of the bar. The U.S.S. *Peacock*, part of Wilkes' squadron, was carried onto the north spit of the river and wrecked. Peacock Spit, named for this early shipwreck, has claimed numerous ships over the years.

The Chinookan People

The Chinookan people—individual tribes that shared a common language—once lived along the embankments of the Columbia River from the Pacific Ocean to the Cascade Mountains. Two of those tribes (Clatsop and Chinook) dwelled at the mouth of the vast river and traded with the early explorers. There are numerous stories of shipwreck survivors being nursed back to health by local tribes, with many sailors assimilating into the culture, living out their days as tribal members.

The Clatsops were ruled in the early 1800s by Chief Coboway, and inhabited the south shore of the river from Tongue Point to Tillamook Head. Coboway made his home where Fort Stevens is now located. Across the river, from the north shore to Willapa Bay, lived the Chinooks. They were governed by the one-eyed Chief Comcomly from his village near the present site of Fort Columbia.

The Columbia River played a significant role in the everyday lives of the inhabitants of the Lower Columbia. Living in the region for thousands of years, they developed the skills necessary to expertly pilot the river's treacherous and unpredictable waters. Proficient fishermen and masterful traders, they employed the river to efficiently conduct business over thousands of miles and with many different peoples. Perfectly situated to barter with traders from the coast as well as the interior, the tribes of the Lower Columbia trafficked in goods from as far away as southern Alaska, northern California and the Rocky Mountains. Chief Comcomly could easily view incoming trade ships from his village above the river, and he personally greeted each one, gaining the captain's favor by bestowing him with gifts, and thus securing his position as master trader of the Columbia.

Salmon was a major source of trade, but canoes, shells, baskets, beads, furs, and slaves were commonly traded as well. Over the years a

A Chinook woman, one of the few survivors of this once populous tribe, circa 1910. Courtesy Northwestern University Library, Edward S. Curtis's 'The North American Indian': the Photographic Images, 2001.

trade language developed—a combination of Chinook, Nootka, English and French. This Chinook jargon was widely used along the coast from California to Alaska until about 1900, giving evidence of the importance of the Chinookan people in Northwest trade relations.

The tribes of the Lower Columbia were separated into four basic social classes—upper class, commoners, free persons, and slaves. Societal mobility was possible, and men and women were ever mindful of rank. At the bottom of the social ladder were the slaves. Slavery was a common practice among north coast tribes. Slaves were either purchased or acquired as captives of war, and often included children kidnapped from distant villages. Slaves were valuable property and a source of labor, performing routine tasks in the village. A wealthy family might own as many as six slaves. When a high-ranking Chinook Indian died, his slaves were put to death and buried under the posts of his raised burial canoe. (4)

James G. Swan, who in the early 1850s lived among the Chinook tribe, described them as "good-looking, robust men, some of them having fine, symmetrical forms," with a complexion that is,

> *much lighter than the Indians of California, or those of Missouri, Alabama, or Florida. The hair of both sexes is long and very black, that of the men hanging loose over the shoulders, while the women, as a usual thing, tie theirs up behind in a sort of a cue, and the young girls braid theirs into two tails, with the ends tied with ribbons or twine. (5)*

The custom of artificially deforming the heads of newborns further differentiated the people of the Lower Columbia from other tribes. Those of high status bound their infants in cradleboards in order to create a flattened head. Infants were wrapped in soft cloth or skins and placed on this board as soon as they were born. A protective cushion was laid on the baby's forehead before adding a wooden headpiece that was firmly secured to the cradle. The child was kept in this position for up to a year, being removed only for exercise or feeding and changing. A naturally formed skull was regarded as a disgrace among the tribes and was permitted only to slaves. A flattened head, on the other hand, was looked upon as beautiful.

The North Coast provided a rich environment that supplied food, clothing, shelter, implements and weapons—dense forests of fir, pine, spruce and cedar, an abundance of game, berries and edible roots, and many species of salmon, shellfish and freshwater fish.

Cedar was essential to the North Coast tribes, not only as material for building their lodges, but also for clothing, utensils and transportation.

Replica of Chinook longhouse at Fort Stevens State Park. Constructed of cedar, these dwellings were often 100 feet or more in length.

The Chinookan people were superb canoe builders, creating 40-foot vessels hollowed out of single logs that they expertly maneuvered through the tricky waters of the Columbia. James Swan described a canoe-builder's precision as he shaped the bottom of a canoe,

> *This he does with no instrument of measurement but his eye, and so correct is that, that when he has done his hewing no one could detect the least defect. . . I saw the progress every day, from the time the tree was cut down till the canoe was finished. This was a medium sized canoe, and took three months to finish it. (6)*

Both banks of the river were dotted with large rectangular homes constructed of huge cedar planks, some as much as one hundred feet or more in length. Multiple families occupied each of these one-room "long houses," which were separated into family compartments by hanging mats or wooden chests filled with supplies. Access to the long-house was a low doorway at one end, usually a round or oval hole that was just large enough to squeeze through. The house was heated by one or more fires running down the center of the house, the smoke escaping through holes in the roof. During the cold, damp Northwest winters, these homes provided a warm retreat. A replica of a long house can be found at Fort Stevens State Park.

For much of the year the women wore only lightweight skirts made from cedar bark or fur, and the men generally went naked. But during the bitter days of winter, the more prosperous donned otter or beaver robes. On rainy days, both men and women wore waterproof conical hats, tightly woven of cedar bark or bear grass.

Nature played a significant role in the religious and philosophical beliefs of the coastal tribes, and their religion focused on guardian spirits and salmon rites. They believed salmon to be a divine gift from the wolf-spirit Talapus, who created the fish to save their people from extinction. Strict traditions honoring Talapus included cutting the salmon lengthwise from mouth to tail (never crosswise against the spine), and returning the bones to the water for rebirth. If the rituals were ignored, harsh punishment, like being buried alive, might result.

Lewis and Clark

The United States purchased the Louisiana Territory from France in 1803, providing the opportunity to explore land west of the Mississippi. President Thomas Jefferson sent Meriwether Lewis, a botanist and intellectual protégé of Jefferson's, and William Clark, a frontiersman and former army captain, to investigate the newly acquired territory. In a letter to Lewis dated June 20, 1803, Jefferson explained his purpose:

> *The object of your mission is to explore the Missouri river, & each principal stream of it, as, by its course and communication with the waters of the Pacific ocean, whether the Columbia, Oregan (sic), Colorado or any other river may offer the most direct & practicable water communication across the continent for the purposes of commerce. (7)*

The Lewis and Clark Corps of Discovery, made up of military men and skilled outdoorsmen, left St. Louis, Missouri, on May 14, 1804. After eighteen months of difficult and dangerous travel across the continent, enduring snow and hail, frostbite and hunger, they spotted what they thought to be a line of breakers in the distance. Clark wrote in his journal on November 7, 1805: "Great Joy in Camp, Ocian (sic) in View, this great Pacific Ocean we have been so anxious to see." They were camped just east of present-day Altoona, Washington, almost twenty miles from the ocean, gazing at the Columbia River estuary.

Their joy at finally reaching their destination was short lived however. The weather conditions on the Columbia were so fierce at the time that, incredibly, it took them over a week to travel the last twenty miles of the river. Five of those days were spent trapped on a rocky shoreline. Stranded by crashing waves, hail and falling rocks, they could do nothing more than huddle together in the driving rain, struggling to keep warm. As they waited for the weather to clear, they named their temporary prison, "Dismal Nitch." Dismal Nitch is located in Washington just east of the Astoria Bridge.

When the weather finally subsided, the party traveled to an area about two miles west of the Astoria Bridge, and on November 15, 1805, they acknowledged their cross-continent trip to be completed. The men constructed a temporary encampment (Station Camp) and attempted to trade with people from a nearby Chinook village. But Chinook Chief Comcomly, a shrewd businessman, was accustomed to trading with large, fully stocked sailing ships and had no interest in the small trinkets in Lewis and Clark's possession. Nevertheless, Lewis and Clark managed to procure a sea otter robe by offering Sacagawea's blue beaded belt in exchange. (8)

In late November, the party crossed to the south side of the river after learning from the Clatsop tribe that elk were plentiful there. They hunted and fished near present-day Tongue Point, before moving to a site along the Netul River (later renamed the Lewis and Clark) where they intended to spend the winter months. Construction of their log structures began in early December, and within three weeks the camp was finished. To honor the local tribe, they named the site Fort Clatsop. In 1805, there were only about four hundred Clatsop people occupying three villages along the river.

By this time Lewis and Clark's supplies were dangerously low, and they were desperate to find someone who could replenish their goods. A trading vessel entered the river shortly after they arrived at Fort Clatsop; however, the local tribe, for whatever reason, failed to tell Lewis and Clark about the ship, or inform the ship's crew about the explorers. Unfortunately, no other ships arrived during their time at Fort Clatsop.

It rained all but twelve of the 106 days they spent at Fort Clatsop, so keeping dry was a continual problem. During the soggy, miserable winter, the party relied on the kindness of the Clatsop people. The Corps of Discovery traded often with the Clatsops, offering fishhooks and bits of cloth in return for skins, roots, dried fish and berries. Relations between the Clatsops and the expedition went relatively well. Although a negative incident occurred the day the corps departed, when they stole a Clatsop canoe. This was more serious than one might think. To Lewis and Clark a canoe meant safe transportation home, but for the Clatsop people a canoe was an integral part of their everyday lives—transporting not only people, but cargo for trade, given as a bride's dowry in marriage, or holding the remains of a loved one who had died. On March 22, while preparing for the return trip home, Lewis wrote the following about Clatsop Chief Coboway:

> To this Chief we left our houses and furniture. He has been much more kind and hospitable to us than any other Indian in this neighborhood. (9)

It is said that for the next ten to fifteen years or so the Clatsops used the fort during hunting season. There is no known record of Chief Coboway's death or place of burial, but all three of his daughters married white settlers.

Fort Clatsop is part of the Lewis & Clark National Historical Park and is located about five miles southwest of Astoria. A community-built replica of the fifty-by-fifty foot fort, erected in 1955, was the focal point of the park for fifty years until it was destroyed by fire on October 3, 2005, just over a month before the planned Lewis & Clark bicentennial. Plans to rebuild and create a more authentic replica of the original fort began immediately, with construction commencing on December 10, the anniversary of the day the expedition began building the original fort two hundred years before. About seven hundred volunteers participated in its rebuilding. The new fort was dedicated a year later on December 9, 2006.

The opening ceremony for the five-day Lewis & Clark bicentennial was held on November 11, 2005, at Fort Stevens State Park, where the Clatsop people originally made their home. Nearly a third of an inch of rain fell during the two-hour event, providing the two thousand spectators an authentic Lewis & Clark experience—rain, hail, winds gusting more than twenty miles per hour, and temperatures in the low forties.

The Lewis & Clark party built Fort Clatsop (replicas pictured here) for shelter during the winter months. It rained all but twelve of the 106 days they spent there. Photo below courtesy Steve Zalewski.

The Fur Trade
1806-1840

Astoria, circa 1811. Courtesy of the Clatsop County Historical Society, Astoria, Oregon, Photo #511-112.

Establishing a Northwest Fur Trade

Before and after the arrival of Lewis and Clark to Fort Clatsop, fur trading continued in the Pacific Northwest just as it had for decades, and vessels regularly stopped to trade with the Chinookan people. During the summer of 1810, the *Albatross* sailed into the Columbia River. The Winship brothers of Boston had dispatched the ship with twenty-four young men aboard to establish a fur company on the banks of the Columbia. After selecting a suitable site near present-day Clatskanie, Oregon, the men set to work building a fortification. Unfortunately, the Chinooks viewed this upriver site as a threat to their trading empire, and wasted no time chasing the men off. The Winship's fur trading establishment, the first on the Columbia River, lasted a mere eight days.

The British Canadian North West Fur Company was constantly on the move and by the early nineteenth century had established trading posts in lower British Columbia, northern Idaho, and in western Montana. After learning about the Lewis & Clark expedition, they made plans to explore the Columbia River, hoping to create a profitable interior trade route to the Pacific. David Thompson, an expert surveyor and explorer of North America, was selected to accomplish this task. In June 1807, Thompson and his party arrived at the headwaters of the Columbia River near what is today Golden, British Columbia. He spent three years surveying and mapping the region. In July 1810, Thompson and a party of about nine men began their quest to follow the Columbia River from its source all the way to the Pacific Ocean. Thompson mapped the route and established trade as he went.

Lewis and Clark also inspired a successful New York fur trader named John Jacob Astor to look toward the Pacific Northwest. Born in Waldorf, Germany, in 1763, Astor emigrated to the United States at the age of twenty-one. He opened a small fur shop in New York City in 1786, and in 1810 Astor organized the Pacific Fur Company with the intention of creating a trading post at the mouth of the Columbia River. Astor hoped to gain control over the entire American fur trade.

Astor planned two expeditions to the Northwest—one by land and one by sea, with both parties expecting to arrive at the Pacific Coast at about the same time. In September 1810, the first group sailed from New York aboard the *Tonquin* under the command of Jonathan Thorn, a seasoned naval officer with a reputation as a rigid and cruel disciplinarian.

The other group left from St. Louis, Missouri, in October on an overland expedition under the leadership of Wilson Price Hunt, a merchant and partner in the Pacific Fur Company. Joining the fifty-six men in this party were Marie Dorion, an Iowa Sioux, and her two children. Astor had hired her husband, Pierre, as a Sioux interpreter.

After sailing around Cape Horn, the *Tonquin* stopped in the Sandwich Islands (Hawaii) to replenish its supply of food and goods, and to purchase livestock. They departed the islands in February with several hogs and goats, two sheep, a quantity of poultry, and a large and diverse supply of vegetables. Captain Thorn also took on two-dozen islanders to help establish the new outpost in the Northwest. Consequently, the earliest Astorians had among their numbers a contingent of Hawaiians who tended the trading post's garden and livestock.

On March 22, 1811, the copper clad *Tonquin* arrived at the mouth of the Columbia River under less than favorable conditions. Eager to be off the ship and establish the trading post, Captain Thorn ignored pleas from his crew that the river conditions were unsafe. The *Tonquin* dipped and yawed in the powerful storm, but Thorn could not be swayed. He ordered Mr. Fox, the chief mate, to take a longboat and four men into the river to locate the channel. As the boat was lowered into the turbulent water, Fox realized his fate and tearfully shouted, "Farewell my friends, we will perhaps meet again in the next world." (1) The small boat was no match for the crashing breakers, and Fox and his entire crew drowned. The next day, Captain Thorn ordered a second boat into the river. All but two men died this time, resulting in a total of eight men lost at sea.

The weather improved, but the ship remained off shore until a suitable site could be found on which to build the trading post. Duncan McDougall and David Stuart scoured the riverbank for a building site, and were returning to the ship when Chief Comcomly cautioned the men not to attempt the eleven-mile crossing. The winds had picked up and the waves were high. But the men, not heeding his warnings, continued on their way. Comcomly trailed a short distance behind them in his large canoe, and when their small boat capsized in the heavy swells Chief Comcomly was there to expertly pull both men from the river, saving their lives, and creating a friendship.

On April 12, 1811, the *Tonquin* safely sailed into the river channel. As the *Tonquin* crew began preparations for constructing the new trading post, the neighboring tribes, inquisitive and eager to trade, hurried about the place. The men decided to call it Astoria in honor of John Jacob Astor, establishing the first permanent European American settlement west of the Rocky Mountains. The trading post was located near present-day Fifteenth and Exchange streets.

Meanwhile, David Thompson and the North West Company continued their way along the Columbia River, reaching Astoria in June 1811, two months after the Americans. How different the history of the Northwest might have been had the British first laid claim to the area.

The Tonquin Disaster

Construction of the new trading post was not moving along as quickly as Captain Thorn would like. Impatient to begin a trading expedition up the coast, he set sail without completely unloading the supplies, thereby leaving the construction crew with limited provisions. Thorn departed for Vancouver Island with a crew of twenty-three and an Indian interpreter.

At Vancouver Island, a chief came aboard to trade with Captain Thorn. But the captain was rude and disrespectful, hitting the chief in the face with an otter skin after a disagreement. The chief's people later returned to the *Tonquin* under the guise of a trading visit. Thorn and his entire crew, save for the ship's clerk, Mr. Lewis and the interpreter, were killed. Although mortally wounded, Lewis hid himself until the next day. When the *Tonquin* was teeming with Indians, Lewis succeeded in firing the ship's store of four and a half tons of gunpowder, destroying the vessel and killing himself and more than one hundred Indians. (2) On a June morning in 1811, the *Tonquin* was gone.

The surviving interpreter escaped from the island and returned to the settlement at the mouth of the Columbia River. His story is the only eyewitness account of the ill-fated *Tonquin*. Canadians call this incident the Battle of Woody Point. In 2003, an eleven-foot anchor thought to be from the *Tonquin* was found off Vancouver Island.

Trading Post Becomes a Fort

After Chief Comcomly plucked McDougall and Stuart from the turbulent waters of the Columbia, the men immediately began amicable trading relations. An alliance developed, and the chief even helped build the new Astoria trading post. But as time went on, Comcomly's

The ill-fated Tonquin *sank in June 1811. A confrontation between its captain and a local Indian chief led to the deaths of nearly the entire crew and more than one-hundred Indians. Courtesy of the Clatsop County Historical Society, Astoria, Oregon, Photo #455-300.*

attitude changed. He sought to ensure his trading monopoly by telling the surrounding tribes that the men at the trading post were cannibals. (3) The Pacific Fur partners wondered why the other tribes, who were so often seen around the post, had disappeared. Fearing they were about to be attacked, the men hastened to secure Astoria. In just a few days they enclosed their dwelling with a fence and built two blockhouses mounted with guns. The traders also began paying an additional markup to Comcomly in order to buy pelts from a hospitable tribe. Eventually, they caught on to Comcomly's scheme, and the Chinooks reluctantly agreed to the traders' prices. To ensure continued friendship and amicable relations with the Chinook tribe, Duncan McDougall married Comcomly's daughter, Ilchee.

As the year went by and the fort's supplies began to dwindle, the men anxiously awaited the arrival of Astor's overland expedition. At last, in February 1812, the bedraggled Wilson Hunt party staggered into Astoria. After losing their way, they had battled sickness, starvation, drownings, hostile tribes, fatigue and desertion. The depleted group reached Astoria seventeen months after leaving St. Louis, with only thirty-five of its original fifty-nine party members. All of their provisions had either been lost or consumed. Hunt wrote in his diary,

> *It was a great delight for travelers overcome with weariness to rest comfortably, surrounded by friends, after such a long journey in the midst of savage people of whom it is always wise to be wary. (4)*

In May 1812, the men at Astoria received reinforcements from another of Astor's ships, the *Beaver*. Ross Cox, who arrived on the *Beaver*, gave the following account of Astoria as it then appeared:

> *The buildings consisted of apartments for the proprietors and clerks, with a capacious dining-hall for both; extensive warehouses for the trading goods and furs, a provision store, a trading shop, smith's forge, carpenter's shop ... the whole surrounded by stockades, forming a square, and reaching about fifteen feet above the ground. A gallery ran around the stockades, in which loop-holes were placed sufficiently large for musketry. Two strong bastions, built of logs, commanded the four sides of the square; each bastion had two stories, in which a number of chosen men slept every night; a six-pounder was placed in the lower story of each, and they were both well provided with small-arms. (5)*

A mural and small replica of Fort Astoria is at the location of the original fort at Fifteenth & Exchange streets. The site was dedicated on September 1, 1956, as part of Astoria's annual regatta celebration. Green diagonal lines on the street mark the outline of the original fort.

War of 1812

Astoria was isolated from the outside world, so it wasn't until January 1813 that they received news of the war with Great Britain. At the time, the fort's supply ship, *Beaver*, having left Astoria in August to trade with the Russians, had not yet returned, so they were without trading goods. The fort was also in no condition for defense, so Astor petitioned the United States government to send a force to protect the post. A ship was dispatched from New York in March 1813 with men and goods for Astoria, but the ship never arrived—it wrecked the following October near the Sandwich Islands.

A replica of Fort Astoria, the first trading post established by the Pacific Fur Company in 1812, located at Fifteenth and Exchange streets.

Instead of getting the reinforcements and supplies they so desperately needed, the men received alarming news. John George McTavish of the British-owned North West Company arrived in Astoria and informed them that a Royal Navy ship was on its way to seize Astoria as a war prize. With no arms and scant provisions, the Astor partners had no choice but to sell out to the North West Company.

On October 16, 1813, the North West Company purchased Astoria for the sum of about $58,000. (6) McTavish offered employment to all of Astor's men and retained Duncan McDougall as second in command. Two months later, the British warship *Raccoon* arrived and would have captured Astoria had it not already been in friendly hands. During a ceremony in December, Astoria was renamed Fort George in honor of the King of England.

April 1814 marked the arrival of the British ship *Isaac Todd*, carrying among its passengers the first governor of Fort George, Donald McTavish. To provide McTavish with comforts of home on the long passage from England, he enticed a young flaxen-haired, blue-eyed (7) Portsmouth barmaid to accompany him. Jane Barnes was her name, and she became the first known white woman to land on the Pacific Northwest coast, arriving thirty years before the females on the wagon trains.

A month after their arrival, Donald McTavish and four others drowned while rowing in the river. Their bodies washed ashore two days later and were buried on the grounds of the fort. The headstone of Governor Donald McTavish is now an artifact of the Clatsop County Historical Society and is on exhibit at the Heritage Museum at Six-teenth & Exchange streets.

Jane, left alone and without her benefactor, caught the eye of Chief Comcomly's eldest son. Enamored by her golden hair, he desperately wished to add her to his collection of wives, offering her friends one hundred sea otter skins for her hand in marriage. Jane flatly refused and would have nothing to do with him. When Jane learned there was a plot to kidnap her as she took her daily stroll on the beach, she quickly fled, boarding a ship bound for China. Jane purportedly made her way back to England.

Treaty of Ghent

The Treaty of Ghent, signed December 24, 1814, provided that all territory and possessions taken by either nation in the War of 1812 were to be returned to the original owner. That meant the British had no choice but to return Fort George to the United States.

By this time the North West Company had firmly established itself in the Northwest fur trade, so Astor abandoned his interest in the trad-ing post. John Jacob Astor never did set foot in Astoria. He returned to the eastern fur trade and to real estate speculation in New York City, becoming the richest American of his time. Worth $2 million in 1810, it is estimated that at the time of his death in 1848 he was worth $20 million—approximately $78 billion in today's dollars. (8)

Although the treaty returned ownership of the fort to the United States, several years passed before the British relinquished control. In 1818, Great Britain and the United States negotiated joint occupa-tion of the Oregon Country, and Astoria continued to be called Fort George until 1846.

Astoria, circa 1841. Courtesy of the Clatsop County Historical Society, Astoria, Oregon, Photo #9278-900.

Hudson's Bay Company

In 1821, the North West Company merged with another British trading operation, the Hudson's Bay Company. Anticipating that the Columbia River would become the international boundary between the United States and Great Britain, the Hudson's Bay Company moved its headquarters ninety miles upriver from Fort George to a site on the north side of the Columbia, at present-day Vancouver, Washington.

Fort Vancouver was constructed in 1825, and Dr. John McLoughlin, a former North West Company physician, was hired to administer the business of the Hudson's Bay Company at the new fort. In so doing, he pilfered most of the equipment and supplies from Fort George.

No longer the headquarters for fur trading, Fort George became nothing more than a lookout station for company ships. Archibald MacDonald, a Hudson's Bay Company official, initially remained in charge of what was left of Fort George. James Birnie took over the post in the mid 1830s, until his retirement in 1845.

Trading ships en route to Fort Vancouver required assistance navi-

gating the Columbia River channel. At the time, the best river navigators were Chinookan men and women, and Chief Comcomly was one
of the most skilled. Hired by the Hudson's Bay Company, Comcomly
became the first official Columbia bar and river pilot. From his perch
above the river, Comcomly had an unobstructed view of approaching
ships. When a ship was sighted, his slaves launched the royal canoe and
delivered him to the incoming vessel. His canoe and its crew were taken
aboard and Comcomly guided the craft upriver to the Hudson's Bay
headquarters at Fort Vancouver.

Attempts at crossing the bar did not always end favorably, however.
In March 1829, a Hudson's Bay Company ship, *William and Ann*, ran
aground, losing all hands. The following morning, the ship's wreckage
littered the beach near the Point Adams Clatsop village. The Clatsop
people immediately began salvaging what they could, as they had been
accustomed to doing for hundreds of years.

When news of the wreck reached McLoughlin at Fort Vancouver,
he dispatched a rescue party to Point Adams. When the expedition
could not find any bodies, rumors began to spread that the crew had
been murdered by the Clatsops. A messenger visited the Clatsop village
demanding that the company cargo be returned and that they reveal
what happened to the crew of the *William and Ann*.

On an afternoon in late June, a company flotilla headed by William
Connolly reached Point Adams. A representative from the Clatsop
village hailed Connolly to tell him that all goods would be returned.
Apparently, at that same moment the winds shifted, putting the ships in
peril. Connolly's men, hurrying to save themselves, jumped into small
boats and headed for shore. Thinking they were about to be attacked,
the Clatsops opened fire. Connolly's men returned fire and continued
ashore, pillaging and burning the Clatsop village.

Disease Takes a Toll

In 1830, "intermittent fever" spread quickly throughout the North
Coast tribes, killing thousands, including Chief Comcomly at the
estimated age of sixty. As per Chinook custom, Comcomly's body was
positioned, along with his most prized possessions, in a burial canoe on
a raised platform. A replica of one of these canoes can be found at the
Astoria Column. It was dedicated by Chief Comcomly's descendants on

Jennie Michel, a Clatsop woman, circa 1900. Courtesy of the Clatsop County Historical Society, Astoria, Oregon, Photo #4299-005b.

April 12, 1961, during Astoria's 150th anniversary.

The native American Indians had no natural immunity to the Europeans' diseases. Between 1830 and 1833, "influenza, typhus, and especially malaria, all brought by the traders, killed seventy-five to ninety percent of the Indians residing below The Dalles of the Columbia." (9) When the Lewis & Clark expedition arrived in 1805, the region was well populated, with approximately 15,000 inhabiting the area along the Columbia River between the Pacific Ocean and Cascade Mountains. "When Lieutenant Charles Wilkes of the United States Exploring Expedition visited the region in 1841, he counted 575 Chinook survivors on the Columbia." (10)

Chief Comcomly's Head

Five years after Comcomly's death, a curious thing happened. Meredith Gairdner, a British physician with the Hudson's Bay Company, determined to make a name for himself by stealing the skull of

Chief Comcomly. In the nineteenth century there was an interest in craniometry—measurement of heads. Believing scientists would be especially interested in the Chinook custom of head flattening, Gairdner considered shipping Comcomly's head to England for scientific study. To make a difficult task even more burdensome, Gairdner was quite ill at the time, suffering from symptoms of tuberculosis. He had already made plans to sail to the Sandwich Islands for his health, and at the last minute, he decided to take the chief's skull with him.

The Chinooks regarded the theft and disturbance of their burial canoes as serious crimes, so Gairdner was aware of the risk he was taking. But when he arrived at the burial place, he found that the chief had been removed from the canoe and buried in a nearby forest, most likely as a precaution against desecration.

Undaunted and beneath the cover of darkness, Gairdner silently crept into the forest in search of the new burial site. Even though he was ill, he was able to find the site, dig up the remains, and decapitate the body without being caught. With bits of skin and hair still attached, Gairdner placed the head in a box and carried it with him all the way to Honolulu. From there he shipped it to his friend Dr. John Richardson at the Haslar Museum at the Royal Naval Hospital in Gosport, England. A year later, Gairdner died of tuberculosis.

Richardson studied the skull for a time and then allowed it to be displayed at the museum where it remained for the next 117 years. The Haslar Museum was destroyed in 1940 during Hitler's bombing of England, but the skull somehow survived, and in 1953 it was given to the Clatsop County Historical Society. Three years later it was loaned to the Smithsonian Institution for study and, finally, in 1972, it was returned to the Chinook tribe. Today, the skull of Chief Comcomly is buried near the site of his native village at the Ilwaco, Washington, cemetery.

Ranald MacDonald

Archibald MacDonald, the man left in charge of the abandoned Fort George, married Princess Raven, a daughter of Chief Comcomly. She gave birth to a son, Ranald, on February 3, 1824, and died soon afterward. Ranald was reared by his father and adored by his Chinook grandfather. It was during his early childhood years that Comcomly was chief bar and river pilot for the Hudson's Bay Company.

Ranald MacDonald grew up on various company posts and, after attending school in Winnipeg, Manitoba, he became a bank clerk. But the life of a clerk didn't provide the excitement he desired, so he devised a plan for adventure. In 1848, at the age of twenty-four, MacDonald climbed aboard the whaling ship *Plymouth*, which was sailing for the Sea of Japan. Having made arrangements with the captain to purchase the ship's twenty-seven-foot sailboat, MacDonald was set adrift near the coast of Hokkaido.

MacDonald had come to believe that the Indians of the Northwest coast were related to the Japanese, and he resolved to carry a message of friendship to the citizens of Japan. Even though foreigners were barred from Japanese soil, MacDonald deliberately capsized his small boat, posing as a castaway. He was picked up and taken under guard to Nagasaki in southern Japan, where he was kept in confinement until he could be sent home on the next western ship.

He was well treated, and during the short time he was there, MacDonald taught English to a class of fourteen interpreters and learned enough Japanese to compile a glossary of English and Japanese words. He remained in Japan for ten months until the naval ship *Preble* arrived in Nagasaki to rescue shipwrecked American sailors. Six years later, on March 31, 1854, when Commodore Perry and the United States Navy began negotiations with Japan, one of MacDonald's Japanese students interpreted for Perry and the U.S. trade delegation.

Japan's first teacher of English spent his last years near Fort Colville, Washington, a former Hudson's Bay post and childhood home. Ranald MacDonald died in 1894 and is buried near Curlew, Washington, close to the Canadian border.

In 1987, members of Friends of MacDonald and the Astoria Rotary Club erected a monument on Rishir Island, Japan, marking the spot where MacDonald went ashore. In 1988, a bilingual monument identifying the birthplace of Ranald MacDonald was erected in Astoria at the site of Fort Astoria at Fifteenth and Exchange streets.

Early Astoria
1840-1860

Fort George, formerly Astoria, circa 1848. Courtesy of Library of Congress, Prints and Photographs Division, [LC-USZ61-497].

Westward Migration

Spanning over half the continent, the Oregon Trail was one of the key overland migration routes on which pioneers traveled to settle in the new western territory. The first person to discover and to follow the entire route of the Oregon Trail was Robert Stuart, one of Astor's partners in the Pacific Fur Company. Stuart arrived in Astoria on the *Tonquin* in 1811, and during 1812-1813 he and his companions traveled the Oregon Trail in reverse, from west to east, a difficult journey that took nearly a year. Along the way, Stuart discovered South Pass, a twenty-mile gap in the Rocky Mountains—a passage accessible to wagon trains.

In 1841, Senator Lewis Linn of Missouri began to annually introduce in Congress a bill that would extend American jurisdiction to Oregon and offer free land to white settlers and "half-breed Indians." Although his Donation Land Claim Act wasn't signed into law until 1850, reports of the immense territory in the West and the possibility of free land had already enticed many to leave family and friends for the unknown.

In May 1843, close to 100,000 gathered in Independence, Missouri, to embark on a grueling trek across virtually unknown territory. The two thousand-mile journey would take six to eight months, and many immigrants would arrive with their resources completely exhausted. Incredibly, there were few deaths along the way.

Encouraged by the success of the 1843 wagon train, more emigrants risked their lives and fortunes for the promise of land in the West. "More than 3,000 traveled overland to Oregon in 1845" (1) and "an estimated 53,000 settlers came to Oregon between 1840 and 1860." (2)

Settling in Astoria

Missionaries were among the first pioneers to arrive in Oregon. In 1840, the Reverend John H. Frost sailed into Astoria on the *Lausanne*, eager to establish a Methodist mission in the area. He chose Clatsop Plains, south of Point Adams, where there were fewer than two hundred Clatsop people, and commenced building a settlement. While Frost's home was under construction, his wife and children lived with the Birnie family in Astoria. At the time, James Birnie was the factor, or agent, for the Hudson's Bay Company at what was left of Fort George. However, Reverend Frost found the Clatsop people reluctant to abandon their beliefs, and he left the mission three years later.

SOL.H.SMITH.   MRS.HELEN SMITH.

Celiast (Helen) Smith, a daughter of Chief Coboway, married Solomon H. Smith, a schoolteacher and prominent settler in Clatsop County. Courtesy of the Clatsop County Historical Society, Astoria, Oregon. Photograph from page 110, Volume II, N. Pacific Hist. Co., Portland, 1889.

Solomon H. Smith, a prominent settler in early Clatsop County, first arrived at Fort Vancouver in the 1830s where he taught school for eighteen months. There he met and later married Celiast, a daughter of Clatsop Chief Coboway. Celiast was first married to a Hudson's Bay Company man, as were many of the Chinookan women. However, many of these men were already married with families waiting for them back in Canada. The men eventually returned to those families, leaving behind their Chinookan wives and any children they had fathered.

In 1840, Solomon and Celiast settled on Clatsop Plains where they established one of the first general stores in the area. Smith is also credited with being the first dairyman in Clatsop County and Oregon's first schoolteacher. In 1874, Smith was elected senator to the state legislature.

The emigration of 1843 brought to Astoria John McClure, John Shively, and A. E. Wilson with land claims filed in Washington D. C. McClure claimed the land from present-day First to Thirteenth streets, Shively from Thirteenth to Thirty-second streets, and Wilson east from Thirty-second.

A bane of present-day Clatsop County was initiated in 1843 when William Hobson settled the Clatsop Plains and sent to England for Scotch broom to beautify his new home. Seeds from those plants soon scattered throughout the county, and before long the shrub was so thick along the roads and highways that the area was given the name "The Golden Trail." (3)

Hobson's son, John, later moved to Astoria where he sold beef and operated a salmon cannery. John's first wife, Diana, was the sister of Dr. Bethenia Owens-Adair, thought to be Oregon's first woman surgeon. (See *Woman Surgeon* in the Boom Times chapter.) John's home, built at 469 Bond Street in 1863, is Astoria's oldest residence to remain in continuous family ownership.

The oldest dwelling in Astoria is the home at 1337 Franklin Avenue that was built in 1852 by Captain Hiram Brown.

In 1846, the same year the dividing line between Great Britain and the United States was established at the forty-ninth parallel, James Welch and his wife Nancy moved to Astoria with their three sons. Soon after their arrival, John Shively asked Welch to look after his land while he traveled to Washington, D. C. to advise the U. S. Congress on matters relating to the dispute with Great Britain over the Oregon Territory. While in Washington, Shively married Susan Elliot. When he and his new bride returned the following year, they found that Welch had claimed their land for himself by occupation, had built himself a house, and was dividing the property into city lots. A lengthy lawsuit followed, ultimately resulting in a compromise with the men agreeing to divide the land between them.

Shively also returned from Washington with a commission as postmaster, opening in 1847 the first United States post office west of the Rocky Mountains. He ran the post office from his home on Fifteenth Street between Exchange and Franklin. This regional center distributed mail throughout the areas now known as Oregon, Washington, Idaho, and Montana, and postage was forty cents. The Shively home was demolished in 1907. A marble obelisk now marks the spot.

In 1847, Samuel Smith and Robert Shortess came to town—Smith settling on the land that is still called Smith Point, and Shortess claiming the area east along the river known as Alderbrook. A barrage of claims continued to be filed, and the 1850 census recorded the population of Astoria as 250.

In 1847 John Shively became postmaster of the first U. S. post office west of the Rocky Mountains. Courtesy of the Clatsop County Historical Society, Astoria, Oregon, Photo #4008-00S.

Export Economy

The California gold rush of 1849 greatly affected the population of Astoria. Some residents left town with dreams of making their fortune in the gold mines, while others were attracted to Astoria by the increased shipping demands on the Columbia River.

A brisk trade had already been established between Astoria and California, but the gold rush and California's subsequent population growth created an increased need for provisions. A growing demand for lumber, wheat, and seafood produced a thriving export economy in the Pacific Northwest.

To satisfy the increasing need for lumber, in 1844, H. H. Hunt and Ben Wood built the first sawmill on the Columbia River. Four years later, James Welch set up the first mill in Astoria at about Ninth and Commercial streets. Lumber had become a large commodity, and by the 1850s Astoria boasted four water-powered mills and Oregon's first steam-powered mill. By 1870, there were 173 sawmills in the state of Oregon. (4)

Employing primitive means, early loggers felled trees of greater girth than most trees harvested today. The highly prized Douglas fir, named for the Scottish botanist who classified it, towered over the forest, reaching heights in excess of three hundred feet, with diameters averaging six feet. These gargantuan trees, among the largest ever seen, crashed to the ground with the use of a simple axe. Once on the ground, a saw was used to cut the trees into approximately sixteen-foot lengths. The smaller logs were laid parallel, creating a "skid road." Oxen were used to "skid" the timber to streams where they could be rafted to the mills. Ross Cox, a clerk with the Pacific Fur Company, sailed from New York to Astoria on the *Beaver*. He arrived in May 1812 and wrote the following:

> *The general size of the different species of fir far exceeds any thing east of the Rocky Mountains, and prime sound pine (spruce) from two hundred to two hundred and eighty feet in height, and from twenty to forty feet in circumference, are by no means uncommon.*
> *(5)*

Though few of those mammoth trees remain in the forests today, a walk through the forested Cathedral Tree Trail in east Astoria gives an idea of how large the trees were hundreds of years ago. The Cathedral

Demand for lumber contributed to a large export economy in the Pacific Northwest. By the 1850s, Astoria boasted five mills. Highly-prized Douglas firs grew in excess of three hundred feet tall. Photograph, circa 1900. Courtesy of the Clatsop County Historical Society, Astoria, Oregon, Photo #633-620.

Logging Scene in a Columbia River Forest, 1890.

Courtesy Library of Congress, General Collections Division, [F583.W53].

Tree itself is a Sitka spruce, which stands about two hundred feet tall and is estimated to be more than three hundred years old. The trail begins at 28th & Irving streets and ends at the Astoria Column.

As commerce created a greater number of ships on the river, so did it cause an increased rate of mishaps. Four major accidents occurred in 1849, and five in 1852, taking sixty-one lives. The tumultuous waters at the mouth of the Columbia soon earned the nickname, "Graveyard of the Pacific."

A Town Divided

The flurry of shipping activity on the Columbia River led to the founding of the first U.S. custom house west of the Rocky Mountains. It was established in Astoria in April 1849. President Polk appointed John Adair as customs collector,

> the duties of the office being to report all vessels arriving at or departing. . . and to keep a diligent watch on the coast to see that none of the Russian or Hudson Bay Companies' vessels came around either for smuggling or trading with the Indians. (6)

John Adair was the first commissioned customs agent on the Pacific Coast and, during his first six months, had jurisdiction over ports in the San Francisco area as well. Customs activities for Puget Sound were also conducted from Astoria until about 1851.

While searching for land on which to build the custom house, Adair lived in the McClure house in Lower Astoria. He attempted to obtain land from several property owners, but no one was willing to either donate land or offer a fair price. In frustration, Adair was forced to build the custom house across Scow Bay, purchasing land from A. E. Wilson. This area became known as Upper Astoria or "Adairsville," (and was later, and still is, called Uppertown). The original custom house burned and was replaced around 1852. A replica of that structure now stands near the site of the original at Thirty-fourth Street and Leif Erickson Drive.

Meanwhile, John Shively and John McClure, having adjacent land claims (known as "Shively's Astoria" and "McClure's Astoria"), were each busily developing separate plans for a future town site. The consequence of their independence is that lot sizes were plotted in differing sizes, so many of Shively's streets did not connect with McClure's

John Adair was the first commissioned customs agent on the Pacific Coast. Photograph, circa 1850. Courtesy of the Clatsop County Historical Society, Astoria, Oregon, Photo #15,549-00A.

streets, and vice versa, resulting in a number of dead ends. There is still evidence of this in Astoria today.

In 1866, John McClure sold his claim (present-day downtown Astoria) to Judge Cyrus Olney and returned to his native Indiana. John Shively remained in Astoria until he died in 1893 at the age of eighty-nine. He is buried in the Greenwood Cemetery on Highway 202.

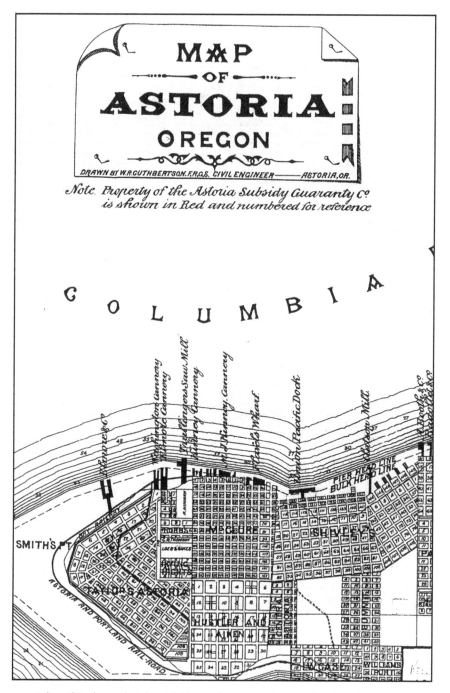

John Shively and John McClure, having adjacent land claims, each developed separate plans for a future town site. Consequently, many of Shively's streets did not connect with McClure's, and vice versa.

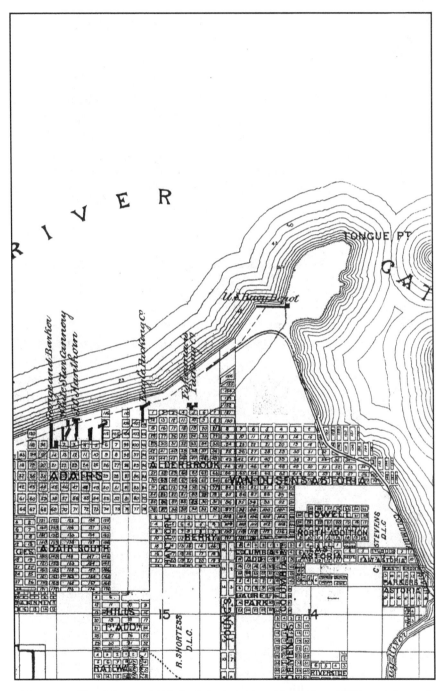

There is still evidence of this in Astoria today. Map, circa 1900, courtesy of the Clatsop County Historical Society, Astoria, Oregon, Photo #89.174.001.

Delivering the Mail

For years Lower Astoria and Uppertown remained separated by Scow Bay, which extended from about Eighteenth Street to Twenty-third Street, creating problems in the day to day lives of Astorians. Around 1853, at the direction of the new postmaster T. P. Powers, the post office was moved from Shively's home in Lower Astoria across the bay to Uppertown. This meant that both the custom house and the post office were now located on the same side of the bay. When residents of Lower Astoria had business to conduct with the customs agent or had letters to mail, the only way to do so was to battle the winds and waves and row across the bay.

In those days there was no mail delivery, so one day in 1855 a local merchant offered to pay William P. Gray a dollar to go to Uppertown and collect his mail. As William was rowing the tiny skiff across the bay, he thought perhaps other people might also be willing to pay him for collecting their mail. William turned out to be quite the entrepreneur, and before long had a large number of customers and was earning $30 a month. (7) William was ten years old at the time, and he continued his mail service for about two years. Captain William P. Gray in later years wrote a letter to a friend saying he believed he had "the first regular rural mail delivery in Oregon. . . and I guess I was the youngest contractor that ever distributed the mail regularly." (8)

With the election of President Abraham Lincoln in 1861, William Adams replaced John Adair as customs collector, and the custom house was moved from Uppertown to Lower Astoria.

In 1873 a new post office was constructed in Lower Astoria at 8th & Commercial streets. Then, from 1878 to 1881, Astoria had two post offices, one downtown and one in Uppertown, which was a separate community. In 1881, the two united into one downtown post office, which operated until 1931, when the building was demolished and a new structure housing the post office and custom house was built on the site. It is still in use today as a post office.

In 1878, a bridge was built connecting the two Astorias, ending thirty years of frustration. The bridge was located at present-day Exchange Street, from about Eighteenth to Twenty-third streets and the town celebrated the occasion with a parade on July 26. However, Uppertown was not included in the official city limits until 1891.

Above: *In 1878 a bridge was built across Scow Bay, ending thirty years of frustration for Astorians. Eventually, the bay was filled in. Photograph, circa 1900. Courtesy Ray Hakala. Below: The first U. S. post office west of the Rocky Mountains opened in Astoria in 1847. Courtesy Salem Public Library Historic Photograph Collections.*

River Transportation

In the early days, transportation across the Columbia River between Astoria and Chinook, Washington, was provided by Chinookan canoe. In 1840, Solomon H. Smith established the first ferryboat service across the Columbia by attaching two canoes together. He transported passengers and freight across the river, weather permitting.

In the late 1840s, a need for passenger service up and down the Columbia River grew. In 1847, a man named B. C. Kindred made his living running a passenger boat from Astoria to upriver points. It took three days to make the trip from Astoria to Oregon City. The fare was twenty dollars, and passengers often found themselves helping to row the boat. (9) Kindred ran a successful passenger boat service until steamers drove him out of business. The first steamship built in Oregon was the *Columbia*. It was built in 1851 in Upper Astoria for John Adair and his partners.

Crossing the Columbia River bar was the first challenge a sailing ship faced when approaching the mighty river. The second was to successfully maneuver the ship through the river's changing channel and shifting shoals. The early sailors had no charts and relied on the Chinookan people to help them cross the dreaded bar and guide them upriver, resulting in many mishaps.

Before 1846, there was no prerequisite for becoming a pilot, so locals without extensive ship handling experience were used in the pilot function. In those days, the pilots did not take control of ships like they do today, but rather offered their knowledge of the river, warning the ship's captain of hazards and suggesting maneuvers.

A portage law was passed in 1846 authorizing the governor to appoint commissioners to examine and license bar and river pilots. The first licensed pilot to work on the Columbia River was Captain S. C. Reeves. During his short career, Reeves made several trips to San Francisco to meet vessels desiring to navigate the Columbia. He lost his life in 1849 when his vessel capsized during a squall.

1850 marked the arrival of twenty-six-year-old Captain George Flavel to Astoria who, within just a few years, created a monopoly on the bar piloting business. In 1851, Captain Flavel became the first licensed Master Mariner to be granted a pilotage license for the bar, bringing his experience and understanding of the capabilities and restrictions of different vessels and their crews.

Above: *Due to the volume of shipping on the Columbia, the first U. S. custom house west of the Rocky Mountains was established in Astoria in 1849. Courtesy of the Clatsop County Historical Society, Astoria, Oregon, Sovey Photo #29.* Below: *A replica of the 1852 building stands near the original site.*

Captain George Flavel's Queen Anne-style home, built in 1885. Courtesy of the Clatsop County Historical Society, Astoria, Oregon, Photo #30,189-965.

In 1865, Captain Paul Corno, intent on competing with Flavel in the piloting business, arrived from San Francisco on the steam tug *Rabboni*. But when Corno's attempts to displace Flavel were unsuccessful, he and his tug returned to California. The use of a tug had proved its value, though, and in 1869 the State of Oregon offered a $30,000 subsidy to anyone who would build and operate a tug at the mouth of the river for five years. Flavel applied for and received the subsidy. He built the tug *Astoria* for $40,000 and placed it into service in December 1869. Before long, Flavel controlled both towage and piloting on the Columbia River.

Captain Flavel was a successful and prominent businessman with an iron will, and,

". . . working men were eager to be employed by him, for, if he exacted the best of service, so, also, did he pay the best of wages, with most gratifying promptness, adding generous commendation when deserved." (10)

Captain George Flavel in the 1850s created a monopoly on the bar piloting business. He eventually became Astoria's first millionaire. Courtesy of the Clatsop County Historical Society, Astoria, Oregon, Photo #531-00Flavel.

Flavel eventually became Astoria's first millionaire. The seventy-three hundred square foot home he built in 1885 for his retirement has been operating as a museum since 1951. Queen Anne architecture is evident in its multiple roof lines, bay windows, three-story tower, fourteen-foot ceilings, and finely crafted woodwork. The home is located on Eighth Street between Duane and Exchange.

Today's bar pilots choose to board incoming vessels via helicopter whenever possible. Otherwise, pilot boats come alongside the underway ship and the pilot climbs aboard by means of a rope ladder attached to the side—an often-precarious procedure, especially when stormy weather produces twenty-five to thirty-foot seas and sixty- to seventy-knot winds.

Maritime Safety

The Pacific Northwest has many coves, inlets and rivers in which to hide, so smuggling became a major problem facing John Adair as the new collector of customs. To remedy the situation, the Treasury Department dispatched the cutter *Jefferson Davis* to Puget Sound in 1854, becoming the first unit of the future United States Coast Guard to be stationed in the Pacific Northwest. Two years later, the *Joseph Lane*, a 102-foot topsail schooner, arrived in Astoria.

In addition to guiding ships over the bar and assisting mariners caught in the river's currents, the *Joseph Lane* enforced the customs laws. Meeting ships offshore, the cutter inspected the cargo and investigated ships suspected of smuggling.

In the mid 1800s, there were no navigational aids to assist sailing ships. Navigators identified headlands from descriptions passed on by earlier sailors, looking for cut trees and white flags, or bonfires at night. The Northwest Coast, noted for its rocky headlands, heavy rainfall, fog, and strong winds was in dire need of navigational aids to prevent further shipwrecks.

The U.S. Lighthouse Service was founded in August 1789, but the first lighthouse in the Pacific Northwest was not completed until 1856 at Cape Disappointment in Washington. In 1853, the bark *Oriole* was arriving with supplies to build the lighthouse when it went aground on a sand bar as it attempted to enter the river. Unable to withstand the current and outgoing tide, the ship was carried out to

An early pilot boat in Astoria Harbor, circa 1885. Courtesy Ray Hakala.

sea, where it filled with water and sank. It was many months before another ship arrived with the needed supplies.

Cape Disappointment is the oldest standing lighthouse in the Pacific Northwest. Its original light was a Fresnel (pronounced "fray-nel") lens. Invented by Frenchman Augustin Jean Fresnel, the lens consisted of concentric rings of glass prisms, and used an oil lantern with multiple wicks, creating a fixed white light that burned constantly from dusk until dawn. The light sat 220 feet above the water and was visible twenty miles out to sea. Purchased for approximately $4,500, it would cost an estimated $6 million to create today. (11) Anticipating that fog would often obscure the light, the builders also installed a sixteen hundred-pound fog bell at the site. But mariners complained that the fog bell was inaudible, so it was eventually discontinued.

In 1862, Cape Disappointment was armed with smoothbore cannons to protect the mouth of the Columbia River from Civil War threats. In 1875, the installation was expanded to become Fort Canby.

Cape Disappointment Lighthouse, built in 1856, was the first lighthouse in the Pacific Northwest. Shown here in 1862 when cannons were added during the construction of Fort Canby. Courtesy of Salem Public Library Historic Photographs Collection.

In 1898, the eleven-foot Fresnel lens was replaced with a smaller, more powerful Fresnel lens, which is still in use today. Where an oil lantern once created a burning white light, one tiny electric bulb now produces Cape Disappointment's alternating red and white lights, which can be seen twenty-two miles out to sea.

The first steam-powered lighthouse tender, *Shubrick*, was built in Philadelphia. Her mission was to carry supplies to the lighthouses and install and maintain buoys and other navigational aids. In 1859 the *Shubrick* set the first buoys in the Columbia River marking the channel from the bar to Astoria.

Vessels approaching from the north had limited visibility of the light from Cape Disappointment, so in 1898 North Head Lighthouse was constructed. Designed by German-born engineer C. W. Leick, it sits two miles north of Cape Disappointment, and its light shines 194 feet above the water. It first used the original Fresnel lens from Cape

North Head is one of the windiest spots on the West Coast. North Head Lighthouse has recorded gusts up to 120 mph. Courtesy Steve Zalewski.

Disappointment and, later, a set of electric beacons. Today, thousand-watt lamps flash a white light every thirty seconds, which is visible twenty-two miles out to sea. This distinguishes North Head Lighthouse from Cape Disappointment's alternating red and white lights. The original Fresnel lens is on display at the nearby Lewis and Clark Interpretive Center.

North Head Lighthouse sits on one of the windiest spots on the West Coast, with recorded gusts up to 120 mph. There is a legend that a head keeper's wife, unable to bear the howling winds, flung herself off the cliff. Both North Head and Cape Disappointment lighthouses are fully functional today, and are under the care of Washington State Parks. Modern electronic and satellite communications and positioning technology have essentially rendered lighthouses obsolete, but the public continues to be fascinated by these historic structures.

By 1885 Astoria had a few dozen homes, one hotel, one church, a saloon or two, and several stores. Shown here is the Occident Hotel, circa 1855. Courtesy of the Clatsop County Historical Society, Astoria, Oregon, Photo #3539-190.

Losing Their Land

Land claims in the early 1840s, the establishment of the Oregon Territory in 1848, and the 1850 enactment of the Donation Land Claim Act were devastating to the native American Indians. The Act granted free land to "every white settler or occupant of the public lands, American half-breed Indians included, above the age of eighteen years, being a citizen of the United States. . ." if they made a claim prior to December 1, 1850. A married man could claim 640 acres of public land, and a single male could claim 320 acres. At the time, there were few white women in the Oregon Territory, so many settlers married Indian women. These women didn't understand that when they married a white man who filed a land claim that they were actually taking land from their own people.

Robert Shortess, sub-Indian agent, wrote from Astoria to the Office of Indian Affairs on November 1, 1850:

> *. . . at first the Indians were promised payment for land taken by settlers, now they are threatened with expulsion from that they still*

The first legal hanging in Clatsop County took place behind this courthouse on December 1, 1893. Courtesy of the Clatsop County Historical Society, Astoria, Oregon, Photo #4022-720.

desire to hold. Consequently they live in a state of continual fear and anxiety, having lost all confidence in our promises and dreading our power. I am myself, I have so long preached patience and hope to them that I am almost ashamed to do so any longer. (12)

In 1851, a treaty was entered into with the Clatsop people. The tribe ceded ninety percent of their land to the U.S. Government, and they were to be paid $15,000 in ten annual fifteen hundred dollar payments. (13) The Tansy Treaty was agreed to and signed by both parties, but it was never ratified, nor did the government honor it. The government, instead, distributed the tribal land to "American" residents.

In 1852, the Chinooks lost additional land when the United States government set aside 640 acres at Cape Disappointment for a future military reservation. Three years later, the tribe was offered a treaty by Washington Territory's Governor Stevens, who had successfully negotiated treaties with other tribes across Washington. The Chinooks rejected the treaty because it would have relocated tribe members from the area where they had traditionally lived.

In 1899, the Chinook, Clatsop, Kathlamet, and Tillamook tribes filed the first lawsuit won by Oregon Indians. They received modest compensation for their lands when their suit was finally settled in 1912.

A Town Slowly Emerges

Astoria was slow to develop—for almost a half-century there were no improved streets, nor were there any docks. Vessels anchored in the river and sent their freight and passengers ashore in small boats. In about 1856, W. W. Parker, having purchased the Welch sawmill, built the first wharf.

Prior to 1849, the Hudson's Bay Company owned the only store in town. It was a crude operation, selling goods from boxes. Adam Van Dusen arrived in the spring of 1849 and reportedly opened the first general store in Astoria where goods were displayed on shelves. The Van Dusen family continues to play a significant role in Astoria today. Adam Van Dusen's great-great-grandson Willis Van Dusen was elected the town's mayor in 1990, and was re-elected to a fifth term in November 2006.

In 1852, 2nd Lieutenant Ulysses S. Grant stayed for a night in Astoria en route to his new post at the Vancouver Barracks. In a letter to his wife, Julia, the young lieutenant gave his impression of the tiny town:

> *Astoria—a place that we see on maps, and read about, is a town made up of some thirty houses... situated on the side of a hill covered with tall trees... with about two acres cleared to give way for the houses. Boats anchoring in the stream (they have no wharf) gives occupation for a few boatmen to carry passengers ashore to see the town that they read about in their young days... So much for Astoria. (14)*

Clatsop County was created by the Oregon Provisional Government on June 22, 1844, and was nearly double the size it is today. County business was conducted in the town of Lexington, near present-day Warrenton, until 1854 when an election was held to select a county seat from among the area's five town sites. "McClure's Astoria" won, most likely because John McClure offered two acres of his land for public buildings. Sessions of the county court were held in private homes while a two-story frame courthouse was being built at Eighth and Commercial streets in Astoria. The first legal hanging in Clatsop County took place behind the courthouse on December 1, 1893. A second courthouse was completed in 1908 on the same site and is still in use today.

Construction of a military road from Astoria to Salem commenced in 1855, and James G. Swan predicted the road would make Astoria "a place of importance, and undoubtedly the largest trading town in Oregon." (15) But the town didn't have much to offer at the time—a few dozen homes, one hotel, a couple of stores, a saloon or two, a small sawmill, a Methodist church, and the post office and custom house. One year later, on January 18, 1856, the Town of Astoria was incorporated by the Oregon Territorial legislature.

Oregon's first school district, established in Astoria in 1854, was School District No. 1. Classes were held at the Methodist church at the corner of Fifteenth and Franklin streets until a school was constructed a few years later. In 1859, the same year Oregon received statehood, Astoria's first public school opened its doors at the corner of Ninth and Exchange streets.

Clatsop County's population in the 1860 census was almost five hundred, and Astoria's population was estimated to be 250, essentially the same number as reported ten years earlier.

Boom Times
1860-1900

Astoria, circa 1867. Courtesy of the Clatsop County Historical Society, Astoria, Oregon, Photo #194-900.

Homesteading

The Homestead Act of 1862 further encouraged settlement in the West by allowing anyone to file for 160 acres of free land. The land would be theirs if at the end of five years they had built a house on it, dug a well, plowed at least ten acres, fenced a specified amount, and resided there. This enticement brought a flood of new immigrants to Oregon.

Although this was good news to the white settlers, native American Indians were dealt a heavy blow. They were not eligible to file claims to their land because they were not considered citizens of the United States. Immigrants moved westward with hopeful hearts at a new life, many settling onto land along the Columbia River—land already inhabited by the Chinookan people. Forced from their native soil, the Chinookan people gradually became separated from one another as they searched for suitable places to live. With no reservation of their own, many of them joined neighboring tribes.

No longer the sleepy little town of the 1850s, Astoria began to grow. In 1870, the population was 639, and ten years later there were more than 1,800 permanent residents and as many as 6,000 during the salmon season. Of course, all of these individuals needed a place to live. It is estimated that between May 1874 and May 1875, at least 100 houses were built in Astoria, and in March of 1877, there were reportedly 189 new buildings under construction. (1)

This unexpected interest in Astoria was mostly due to the developing canning industry, although river commerce was gaining momentum as well. In 1874, the Astoria and Willamette Barge Company was created to transport wheat from farms in the Willamette Valley to vessels at Astoria. By 1875, there were approximately eighty-five foreign-bound vessels in the Columbia River fleet. (2)

Preparing for Defense

Another project that attracted new residents to Astoria was the construction of the two forts on opposite sides of the Columbia River. After the boundary conflict between the United States and Great Britain was settled in 1846, and the Mexican-American War ended two years later, the United States took measures to defend its new territory. In 1852, after surveying sites at the mouth of the Columbia River, lands on Cape Disappointment and Point Adams were set aside for possible military purposes—Cape Disappointment being the north entrance to the Columbia, and Point Adams being the south.

Ten years later, following the outbreak of the American Civil War, officers of the Corps of Engineers surveyed the sites and made recommendations for the forts. Construction of Fort Canby at Cape Disappointment began in the summer of 1862. It presented quite a challenge, though, because the main point of defense was at the lighthouse, which stands over two hundred feet above the sea. Fort Stevens, developed at the former Clatsop village at Point Adams, was ready for occupancy three years later.

By the late 1800s, both Fort Stevens and Fort Canby had been virtually abandoned and were in dire need of repairs and modernization. Around 1895, the War Department made preparations for a mining facility at the river entrance and for the erection of batteries on land acquired decades earlier at Chinook Point (site of Chief Comcomly's former village). In an intensive construction program that began in 1896, Fort Stevens was remodeled and reactivated, Fort Canby's Civil War era armaments were replaced, and new construction began at Chinook Point—named Fort Columbia in 1899. The mouth of the Columbia was now deemed safe, as each fort had arcs of overlapping fire, yet each fort was out of range of the others—so if the enemy captured one fort, other forts would still be safe.

These three forts remained essentially unchanged until World War II, when the numbers of troops at each of the forts increased. But in 1947, Fort Stevens, Fort Columbia, and Fort Canby were all listed by the War Department as surplus property. A year later, 491 acres of Fort Canby was transferred to the U. S. Coast Guard, becoming Coast Guard Station Cape Disappointment.

The Big Cheese

At the outbreak of the Civil War, women searched for ways to be of service, such as sewing clothing for soldiers. This simple idea led to the founding of a national sanitary commission. Approved by President Lincoln in June 1861, the commission acted in accord with the medical bureau and sought ways to supplement what the government was providing for its troops. Expert physicians inspected camps, taking into consideration their location, general cleanliness, methods of cooking, etc. and filed reports with the commission. The collection of personal supplies for the soldiers was left largely to branches in which women were prominent. Items such as quilts, butter, eggs, cider, and chickens were gathered and packaged. The standard set for the local-aid societies was "a box a month for the soldiers." (3)

During the summer of 1862, the State of Oregon called on each of its counties to make a contribution to the Sanitary Commission. It was suggested that Clatsop County, being known at the time as a dairy region, provide a giant cheese. Dairyman John Hobson and his sister-in-law Bethenia Owens took up the challenge and succeeded in creating a mammoth round of cheese by using a hog's head as the frame. After selling the cheese several times at auction in Astoria, where it raised $145.00 (4), it was placed on exhibit at the Oregon State Fair in Salem. The cheese and the proceeds, which reportedly were between four and five hundred dollars (5), were to be sent to soldiers in the field.

Much of the money raised by the Sanitary Commission was by means of fairs, some lasting for weeks. During its existence, the Sanitary Commission received almost $5 million in monetary donations and approximately $15 million in supplies nationally. (6)

Fishing the Columbia

Columbia River fishermen competed for their fair share of the salmon harvest by employing various fishing methods. Fish wheels, fish traps, and horse seines were used, operating in locations where fish regularly appeared. Powered by the river current, the fish wheels scooped the migrating salmon into a storage bin. When the bin was full, the wheel's operator climbed down a ladder, speared the fish with a long pike, and skillfully dropped the fish into a small hand-cranked elevator, which hoisted the fish above the deck. Trap fishing was an easy fishing method, as the salmon would simply swim into an enclosure of web from which they could not escape. Placed at the mouth of the river, these devices could capture a considerable number of fish as they swam upstream. Seine fishing demanded the muscle of twenty to forty men driving teams of horses. Most effective at low tide, one end of a seine was anchored on the beach while a team of horses pulled the loose end through the water. All of these fishing methods were eventually outlawed in Oregon when it was determined that fish runs were thinning.

Gillnets were used on the Columbia River as early as 1853 and are still in use today. In the early days, a gillnet consisted of a rectangular piece of linen and, later, nylon webbing, that was weighted on the bottom and buoyed on the top by a string of corks. The webbing was laid across a stretch of river, and as it drifted with the current the salmon's gills became entangled in the web. It was an efficient, albeit hazardous way to fish, because in the early days fishing took place in the dark to prevent fish

Above: *Built in 1897, the Union Fisherman's Net Drying Loft still stands on its original pilings in the river. This photo was taken before the building sustained incredible damage during the Storm of 2007.* Below: *An early "butterfly" fishing fleet, circa 1900. Courtesy of the Clatsop County Historical Society, Astoria, Oregon, Photo #5393-315.*

Astoria and the mouth of the Columbia River, circa 1880s.

from seeing the cotton webbing. Under cover of darkness, hundreds of boats maneuvered the fickle waters of the Columbia. In 1874, disaster struck when an unexpected squall took the fishermen by surprise, leaving twenty-six dead. During the peak salmon years, several thousand gillnetters vied for a section of the river. The early gillnetters became known as the "butterfly fleet" because of the distinctive wing-shaped sails on their boats.

Fishermen would often make or mend their nets during the winter months. Made of natural fiber, the nets needed to be dried between uses. One building, constructed for this purpose in 1897, is still standing on its original pilings in the river. Located at about Thirty-first Street, this net drying and mending loft enabled fishermen to navigate their boats under the building where a hoist would lift the nets to dry.

In 1879, gillnet fishermen formed the Columbia River Fishermen's Protective Union with representatives up and down the river. With so many boats competing for the same area, the union's main purpose was to maintain order and reduce safety hazards. The union went through multiple reorganizations during the next two decades as the number of Columbia River fishermen continued to grow. It is estimated that in 1888 there were 1,400 boats and 2,800 fishermen working on the river. (7) Fishing on the Columbia was hazardous duty. During the 1893 season alone over one hundred men lost their lives. (8)

Spring chinook was the mainstay of the Columbia River canning industry in the late 1800s. During the salmon season, when Astoria's population skyrocketed, there often weren't enough accommodations for everyone. The population in 1876 reached 2,500, and soared to 6,000 in 1880. The 1880 census for Clatsop County listed 1,293 fishermen, ninety percent of whom were single, with six out of seven living in boarding houses. Some men, and even a few families, resorted to living on the river in makeshift residences called "scow houses." A tent or a crudely constructed shack was positioned on a barge tethered to a dock or street. It must have been a sight to behold. D. C. Ireland described it like this:

> ... the bigger ones had entire families living on them and it was a common sight to see women hanging out their washing on lines fixed far below the surface of the street. These women would try and spruce up their homes with curtains and such truck, but it must have been a struggle to keep things neat because of the debris which came down on them from above at all hours, not to mention the occasional drunk who lost his footing and plummeted down into someone's bedroom at the midnight hour. (9)

News of the prolific salmon industry lured men to Astoria from all parts of the world. Many came from Scandinavia and, in particular, Finland. Most of Astoria's fishermen of Scandinavian descent resided in Uppertown and Alderbrook, and a large Finnish population settled in what is still known as "Uniontown," so called because of the Union Packing Company that was built there in 1881. Uniontown covers an area of roughly thirty blocks, and was also referred to as "Finn Town." At one time Astoria had two Finnish-language newspapers. Each year near the summer solstice Astoria celebrates its Scandinavian heritage with a Midsummer Festival.

Columbia River Canneries

The first Pacific salmon cannery was established in 1864 in California, where brothers William and George Hume, and their friend Andrew Hapgood, revolutionized the technology of preserving fish by replacing salting with canning. Each individual can was processed by hand with the salmon packed in salted water and boiled to 230° F for one hour. Their business flourished until 1866, when the salmon run in the Sacramento River proved inadequate to meet the company's demands. As a result, the company relocated to the Columbia River where salmon was plentiful.

Hapgood, Hume and Company built the first Columbia River salmon cannery about fifty miles upriver at Eagle Cliff, WA. The canning process, which allowed the long-distance transportation of fish at inexpensive prices, sparked an immediate interest in canning that led to decades of prosperity in the region. Early cannery owners fared well, quickly realizing immense profits on their ventures. In the 1880s, salmon reportedly sold for fifty cents a pound in New York City. (10)

Astoria soon became the center of salmon canning operations. The first Astoria cannery was Badollet & Co., opening in 1874 (Thirty-third & Leif Erickson Drive). A year later, Booth & Co., located a block west, was the second Astoria cannery. J. O. Hanthorn & Co. soon followed, building a cannery at the east end of town. Located at Pier 39, it is the only remaining cannery building in Astoria. By 1877, the town had nine canneries in operation, and ten years later nearly two dozen lined Astoria's riverfront.

The first cannery built in the downtown area was the Kinney Cannery. Built in 1876 between Fifth and Sixth streets, it became one of the most successful canneries in Astoria, packing 67,000 cases in 1891. (11) The building burned in 1894, but was rebuilt on its original supports. It is rumored that large mounds of melted cans from the fire could be seen beneath the building. The building was placed on the National Register of Historic Places in 1989. Unfortunately, in December 2010, the building burned to the ground once again.

The Samuel Elmore Cannery, the oldest continuously operated salmon cannery in Astoria, opened along the Columbia River in 1881. Courtesy of the Clatsop County Historical Society, Astoria, Oregon, Sovey Photo #112.

The Samuel Elmore Cannery, the oldest continuously operated salmon cannery in Astoria, opened along the Columbia River in 1881 (just east of the Astoria bridge). In the early days, the Elmore Cannery was one of the best-equipped operations on the Pacific Coast, at one time employing 350 fishermen and 100 cannery workers. In later years, Bumble Bee Seafoods operated the cannery, canning both salmon and tuna. The building was designated a National Historic Landmark in 1966. It closed in 1980, and the building was destroyed by fire in 1993.

By 1881, thirty-five canneries dotted both sides of the Columbia River, and just two years later the number had risen to fifty-five. (12) In 1883, the canneries packed a whopping 630,000 cases of chinook salmon, two-thirds of the entire Pacific Coast production. (13)

There seemed to be an unending supply of salmon in the 1880s, and the fishermen hauled in so many that the canneries were unable to keep up. Even running long hours didn't help. "Forty Chinese workers at Devlin's worked full time making tin cans, reportedly 17,000 per day in 1882, and this was not enough." (14) When all available tins were filled, the remaining salmon were simply tossed back into the river—hundreds of forty- to fifty-pound fish each day. The dead fish returned to the beach with the changing tide, and sometimes bear and cougar were seen eating the remains. The stench from rotting fish wafted into town, so citizens with skiffs were hired to haul the rancid fish farther out into the channel. This was in the March 22, 1885, issue of *The Daily Astorian*:

> *. . . Last summer it stunk the whole time; a little effort would do away with the nuisance and furnish what Astoria badly needs—a place to take a drive or pleasant stroll in leisure hours.*

This wasteful practice of throwing fish away eventually affected the fish runs. The canneries often processed only the highly-prized chinook salmon, so many complete species were discarded. Artificial propagation began in 1887, and legislation was passed in 1888 restricting fishing. However, in 1895, the U.S. Commission of Fish estimated that seven million pounds of fish were still being discarded every year.

In the late 1890s, with the realization that fish runs were thinning, seven canning companies joined forces, forming the Columbia River Packers Association. It was comprised of ten canneries along the Columbia River and a large plant in Bristol Bay, Alaska. Participating owners were either bought out or given stock equal to the value of their canneries and their land. The Association centralized its operations, using the Samuel Elmore plant as the main cannery with the other cannery locations being used for office space or cold storage.

Chinese Cannery Workers

The emergent salmon industry employed hundreds of laborers. Fishermen supplying the canneries were mostly of European descent. The Chinese were not allowed to fish, but because they provided cheap labor, most canneries employed them to process the fish. Chinese immigrants first came to the United States in the 1850s in an effort to escape harsh economic and political conditions back home. Finding work in the gold mines of California, helping to build railroads, and working the retail trades in areas like San Francisco, the Chinese toiled diligently.

George Hume in 1871 was the first to hire Chinese cannery workers. Before the canning boom of the 1870s only a handful of Chinese lived in Astoria, most finding employment as cooks, dishwashers, wood choppers, levee builders, or servants in European-American homes.

News of the pending 1882 Chinese Exclusion Act, which would ban the immigration of Chinese laborers for ten years, created an immediate emigration surge from China to the United States, with many finding their way to Astoria. By 1887, several thousand Chinese were

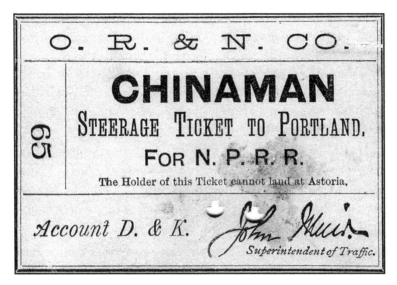

At one time, unemployed Chinese were not welcomed in Astoria. One-way steerage tickets to Portland were stamped with "CHINAMAN" and read: The Holder of this Ticket cannot land at Astoria. Courtesy of Ray Hakala.

employed in the town's canneries, and Astoria had its own Chinatown. However, because of the Exclusion Act, by 1900 the average age of the Chinese cannery worker was nearly forty-five.

When the Exclusion Act expired in 1892, Congress extended it for another ten years, and it was made permanent in 1902. Then, in 1943, when China was an important ally of the United States against Japan in the Second World War, Congress repealed the Act.

Some white residents resented the Chinese in Astoria, and there were instances of discrimination and persecution. Chinese men were excluded from fishing jobs, which were held primarily by Euro-American immigrants. Various prejudicial ordinances were passed by the city council, such as a law banning the Chinese custom of carrying baggage attached to a pole. Numerous Chinese were arrested for violation of this law. In spite of the persecution, Chinese immigrants felt relatively safe in Astoria when compared to other western towns where open race wars were common. Most Astorians refrained from anti-Chinese activities, fearing the laborers might abandon the canneries, causing the collapse of the local economy.

There was a time when the Chinese were not welcome in Astoria unless they were employed at one of the canneries. One-way steerage tickets to Portland were often issued to the Chinese, stamped "CHINAMAN," that indicated: "The Holder of this Ticket cannot land at Astoria."

Chinese cannery workers handled the fish every step of the way—from unloading the fish onto the docks, to filling and testing each can. Butchers were at the top tier of the crew's internal hierarchy, as were can makers and can testers. These positions were essential to a cannery's success and they received the best pay and highest status. The work was fast-paced, and a highly talented butcher might handle between seventeen hundred and two thousand fish a day, or fifteen to eighteen tons.

At the lower end of the ladder were the graders and fillers. In the late 1870s when canners began to put up other kinds of salmon besides the prized chinook, a grader's ability to identify the salmon was crucial. Graders deftly flipped salmon into the appropriate bins with gaff hooks in each hand, requiring great strength and stamina.

The simple task of filling the cans was not easy work by any means, and in fact could be quite hazardous. Sharp bones, can edges, and knives often caused cuts and infections. Fillers withstood swollen wrists and fingers, battled skin rashes and fevers, and in rare cases the horrifying loss of fingers or even a hand.

In the early days, men predominated in Chinese immigration. Cannery owners discouraged the presence of families and only reluctantly accommodated contractors and foremen. Chinese contractors hired, fed, housed, and paid laborers for cannery companies but provided low wages, substandard housing, and poor food. Most contractors lived permanently in Portland or San Francisco, and only temporarily in Astoria. The 1880 census listed nearly thirty-one percent of Chinese cannery workers as married, but none had wives with them. The contract system for hiring cannery workers ended shortly after World War II.

All of the cannery men worked long, harsh hours, ten or eleven hours a day, six days a week. Some sought relief from the pains of their tedious work, and opium addiction was commonplace in Chinatown.

Canneries were built side-by-side on the waterfront with Chinese bunkhouses directly behind and beneath the street. The only source of heat in these one- and two-bedroom structures was a single coal or wood-burning stove. May Spexarth Miller recalls visiting the Chinese living quarters in about 1906 with her father:

> For blocks, on Astor and Bond, there were closely built wood one-story houses or shops. . . all just above the tide coming in and going out each day. . . I can well remember the incense burning and opium smoke and dried fish odor and I couldn't eat lunch that day. The odor

Above: *By 1887 several thousand Chinese were employed in Astoria's canneries, working long, harsh hours. Courtesy of the Clatsop County Historical Society, Astoria, Oregon, Photo #5613-330. Below: Salmon canning. Courtesy Library of Congress, Prints and Photographs Division, [LC-USZ62-95113].*

and the thought of those families living down under the sidewalks
really got to me. (15)

The Chinese depended on one another for security resulting in the formation of tongs, political parties, and religious organizations. Forming these associations was one way the Chinese adapted to their often-hostile environment. A tong was essentially an American invention, similar to a fraternal organization. They were organized by Chinese residents to help newly arriving Chinese adjust to life in America. In addition to the tongs with social, political, and cultural associations, there were those that depended heavily on the vice industry for income—keeping Chinese laborers in a state of indebtedness through gambling, drug trafficking, and prostitution. In 1888, violent confrontations erupted in the competition for gambling in Astoria.

Chinese cannery workers seldom received more than a basic subsistence, so their leisure activities included gathering additional food. The Chinese collected and used dried seaweed in soups and for medicinal purposes, and they regularly ate perch, flounder, sole and low-grade salmon caught by fishermen or themselves. Some workers harvested and processed wapato, a root long used as a staple by the coastal Indians, and a few kept small gardens.

On their one day off each week, the Chinese spent time in various social activities such as celebrating holidays and festivals, or building and flying kites. They expertly constructed all kinds of kites, some emitting musical notes, and others so large they required the assistance of at least a dozen men. In the late 1890s, when Astoria began to celebrate its regatta, the town's annual event marking the importance of the fishing and canning industry, Chinese took part in the festivities. The concentration of Chinese in Astoria also attracted a Chinese theater troupe. As early as 1881, Chinese operas ran every other night during the canning season. By 1883, Astoria's Chinese residents had a theater of their own.

Beginning in 1905 the Smith Butchering Machine replaced Chinese laborers in many canneries, particularly those in Alaska, where salmon were most plentiful. These machines were offensively referred to as "Iron Chinks" because they could gut, cut, and clean salmon at a rate equivalent to thirty or forty skilled Chinese workers. Most of the Chinese eventually left Astoria, but those who remained found success in other businesses such as laundries, barbershops, restaurants, and gardening. And many began to marry, generating a shift in the character of the community from one of young migrant bachelors to a community with families.

On May 17, 2014, Astoria hosted a grand opening of the Garden of Surging Waves, an interpretive park designed to honor Astoria's Chinese heritage. The park is located at the corner of 11th & Duane Streets, includes artwork from China, and is the anchor piece for a proposed Astoria Heritage Square. The Chinese written characters for the words "surging wave" are also used to express hardship and struggle — experiences shared by many of America's early immigrant groups.

Newspaper Man

As more and more people settled in Astoria, businesses flourished, and the town required a newspaper. The *Marine Gazette* was the first newspaper published in Astoria, established in 1864 by James Newton Gale. Short lived and folding after only two years, Astoria then went without a newspaper until DeWitt Clinton Ireland founded the *Astorian* at the behest of Adam Van Dusen. Ireland was an experienced newspaperman, having founded his first newspaper at the age of nineteen in Mishawaka, Indiana. After moving to Oregon, he established the *Oregon City Enterprise*. Ireland actually started the *Enterprise* with equipment he purchased from the fallen *Marine Gazette*.

The first issue of the *Astorian* was published on July 1, 1873, and the paper has been in continuous operation since. Beginning as a tri-weekly publication, at different times it was published weekly, or daily, depending on the financial situation of the paper. After Western Union completed a telegraph line to Astoria, making it possible to receive regular news dispatches, *The Daily Astorian* made its first appearance on May 1, 1876.

Ireland was instrumental in transforming Astoria into a respectable town. He was twice elected mayor, and while in office passed several important ordinances. Perhaps one of the most significant problems he addressed was the town's offensive odor. Most of Astoria's buildings and houses sat on pilings over the river, and their outhouses emptied directly into the river below. Add to that the town's garbage that was regularly dumped over the sides of the docks, and the incessant waste from the canneries, and one might well imagine the resulting stench. Ireland passed an ordinance that prohibited outhouses, slaughterhouses, cesspools, and the like in the downtown area.

D.C. Ireland also had a hand in securing Astoria's first hospital. There were one or two physicians living in town, but their skills were reportedly inferior. In addition to treating the town's residents, there were often injured or sick seamen requiring care. After the death of his eleven-year-

The Wide West. *Courtesy Salem Public
Library Historic Photograph Collections.*

old son, Ireland began an editorial campaign urging the townspeople to
build a hospital.

In 1880, the Sisters of Charity purchased the Arrigoni Hotel and,
after a bit of remodeling, established St. Mary's Hospital in Astoria.
Ireland wrote the following in his newspaper in July 1880:

> . . . *The buildings and the grounds are well located for the purpose,
> and we doubt not that many invalids from the interior will be
> glad to avail themselves of the advantages and benefits such an
> institution offers, where they will receive the very best of medical
> treatment and care, combined with the well-known bracing effect
> of a healthy sea breeze. This hospital was one of the needs of
> Astoria. It is supplied sooner than we anticipated.*

The hospital was located at Fifteenth and Exchange streets. It was
added onto in 1895, and in 1905, a new building was constructed on the
site, which would later include a nursing school. A newer, brick building followed, and remains today as the Owens-Adair Apartments. (See
Woman Surgeon later in this chapter.)

When D. C. Ireland was mayor he welcomed several prominent individuals to Astoria. Ulysses S. Grant made a second visit, this time as

Above: *After moving to Oregon, D. C. Ireland established the* Oregon City Enterprise *and subsequently the* Astorian. *He was twice elected mayor of Astoria. Courtesy of the Clatsop County Historical Society, Astoria, Oregon. Photograph from Astoria Library. Below: St. Mary's Hospital, circa 1912. D. C. Ireland launched an editorial campaign in his newspaper to build a hospital after the death of his young son. Courtesy of the Clatsop County Historical Society, Astoria, Oregon, Photo #9223-565.*

General Grant, and in October 1880, President Rutherford B. Hayes and General William Sherman arrived aboard the *Wide West*. They were greeted by the town's band, and a large reception was held in their honor at the Occident Hotel. President Hayes told Ireland that he thought Astoria and the area looked prosperous and progressive. (16)

The Ireland marriage was apparently on shaky ground after the death of their son, and his wife, Olive, filed for divorce. DeWitt Clinton Ireland left Astoria, selling the *Astorian* and the building in 1881 to J. F. Halloran and P. W. Parker for $8,000 in gold coins. (17)

On the Wild Side

Astoria had quite the nightlife in the 1870s and 1880s, most likely because the town was teeming with transient fishermen and cannery workers who had pockets full of money and no families to support. Astor Street was Astoria's red light district, lined with gambling houses, opium dens, brothels, and taverns. Rumored to be one of the finest red-light districts in its day, prostitutes of many ethnic backgrounds came purposely for the canning season, when Astoria's population of men increased considerably. A Portland newspaper described Astoria during the canning season as "the most wicked place on earth for its population." (18)

A plethora of saloons sprang up between Fifth and Tenth streets, and the area became known as "swill town." As Astoria's population grew, so did the number of saloons. In 1875, Astoria had twenty-seven saloons, and at least two breweries to supply them. (19) "Over one-third of the town's income in 1880 came from city-mandated liquor license fees." (20)

One of the most successful breweries in Astoria was the North Pacific Brewery in Uppertown. Constructed in 1896, the building was the most expensive in Astoria at the time, costing $56,000, and containing $100,000 in equipment. Beer production began in December of 1896 with an output of two hundred barrels a day. (21) For the 1903 Astoria regatta, the North Pacific Brewery created a special "Regatta Beer."

The brewery was eventually closed by Prohibition in 1915, and then from 1928 until 1960 it was a working fire station. Located at Thirtieth and Marine Drive, it is now home to the Uppertown Firefighter's Museum, with fire equipment on display dating from 1877-1963.

In 1896, a Finn by the name of August Erickson opened a three-story saloon called The Louvre, at Seventh and Astor streets. The *Daily Morning Astorian* reported The Louvre "the most elegant drinking place in

Above: *The North Pacific Brewery began beer production in December of 1896 with an output of two hundred barrels per day. Courtesy of the Clatsop County Historical Society, Astoria, Oregon, Photo #6984-400B.* Below: *The Daily Morning Astorian reported The Louvre "the most elegant drinking place in Astoria." The Louvre boasted a billiard hall, orchestra pit, public bar, arcade, and even a roller skating rink. Courtesy Ray Hakala.*

Astoria." The Louvre boasted a billiard hall, orchestra pit, public bar, an arcade, and even a roller-skating rink. Items from the original saloon are on display in the Heritage Museum at Sixteenth & Exchange.

Records indicate that city administrators made several attempts to enforce orderly conduct in the "wide open town." For example, women were forbidden to work in bar rooms or drinking shops (thanks to D. C. Ireland) and in 1887, an ordinance was passed prohibiting three or more persons from standing together on the sidewalk, lest they obstruct the passage of vehicles and passengers. Offenders were reportedly fined up to fifty dollars or were confined in jail twenty days. (22) Saloons and other places of entertainment were required to be closed between midnight and five a.m. Firearms were illegal within the city limits as early as 1856.

A police report dated October 16, 1883, describes what may be the first speeding ticket issued in Astoria: "Alfred Shepardson was arrested for violating ordinance 195 by driving a horse faster than four miles per hour." One might wonder how the officer clocked Mr. Shepardson's speed.

Shanghaied

A history of Astoria would not be complete without mentioning the infamous practice of "shanghaiing," or "crimping." To shanghai someone was to kidnap a man for a forced term of labor aboard a ship, or to trick him into signing a sea-faring contract. The law considered any sailor who had not soberly agreed to these contracts as having been shanghaied.

Maritime working conditions in the days of sailing ships were poor at best, and a shortage of sailors was a problem in many countries. The practice of crimping may have begun as early as the seventeenth century when British press-gangs working for the government obtained sailors for the royal navy by means of violence, kidnapping and trickery. This practice soon spread to other countries.

In Astoria, crimps often targeted young, inexperienced men who were new in town. Sailor runners from ships in the harbor would often shanghai men at night by simply knocking them over the head. Cannery workers began carrying loaded revolvers when traveling to and from their jobs. Monte Hawthorn, who worked in an Uppertown cannery in the 1880s, described what it was like to walk to work in the dark:

I'd walk careful-like with my hand on my revolver. And, do you know, every fellow that I met on that stretch done the same thing. We'd

Bridget Grant with her children, circa 1900. Owner of a boarding house for seamen, Bridget and her sons often sold men to shanghaiers. County Folklore says she even had her husband shanghaied to avoid a divorce. Courtesy of the Clatsop County Historical Society, Astoria, Oregon, Photo #8665-00G.

pass with our hands on our hips, turned side-ways, keeping our eyes on each other, and sometimes backing up as we walked away. (23)

Crimps sometimes used more elaborate means to shanghai men. Alfred Clark related a personal account of an incident in 1891 to *The Oregonian* newspaper. After accepting an invitation to a party aboard a riverboat in Portland that included a cruise to Astoria, he and the other passengers were treated to a tour of a sailing ship. To be assured of their return passage to Portland, they were told to write their names on what they thought was a passenger list. Once aboard the sailing ship, however, they learned they had all signed a copy of the ship's articles which, when properly signed, was a legal document. Mr. Clark spent four months aboard the *T. F. Oaks*, and oddly enough, eventually became a career sailor.

There is the story of an Astorian crimp named Paddy Lynch who traveled to Tacoma, Washington, with the intention of recruiting sailors, only to find himself shanghaied. He somehow managed to get away when the ship reached San Francisco. Lynch was later sent to prison for shanghaiing, and at the time of his release in 1906, crimping was a thing of the past—no doubt because sailing ships were being replaced with steamships, which required skilled workers.

Near Commercial and Fourteenth streets was a boarding house for seamen owned by Bridget Grant, who arrived in Astoria in 1876. She and her sons often sold men to shanghaiers, and county folklore says that Bridget even had her husband shanghaied to avoid a divorce. The story continues with her husband returning a few years later, tripping on a dock and drowning. Bridget died in Portland in 1923 at the age of ninety-two.

"Shanghaied in Astoria," a production of the Astor Street Opry Company, stars local actors and lightheartedly re-enacts the shanghai days of old Astoria. It has been running every summer since 1985.

Fire of 1883

On July 2, 1883, a fire ignited at the Ferrell sawmill at about Fourteenth and Exchange streets. The flames spread quickly to the surrounding blocks, destroying all structures on Commercial Street between Fourteenth and Seventeenth, including the wooden streets and sidewalks.

At the time of the fire, the city of Astoria was flourishing and had one of its most successful years in the cannery business, packing 630,000 cases of salmon. But all of downtown was built on wood pilings over the water, providing plenty of tinder-dry fuel. There were also no fire hydrants to help extinguish the flames, and the town's two steam fire engines and hook and ladder wagon were no match for the rapidly advancing fire.

Looting created a major post-fire problem, and the police appeared helpless to do anything. A newspaper story described the mayhem:

The burning of the Foard & Stokes store furnished an example of depravity we would prefer not chronicling: brutes in human shape stood there stealing, breaking open case liquors, guzzling down wine, and throwing provisions to their comrades in boats below. (24)

A vigilance committee quickly formed with the intention of recovering the stolen merchandise and arresting those responsible. Once the committee identified the first man, the vigilantes ordered the sheriff and chief of police to stand aside. They escorted the man to the cemetery, where they gave him a swift trial, finding him guilty of possessing stolen property. He was then given a choice of punishments—hanging or whip-

Above: *Fire of 1883 destroyed most of Astoria's downtown. Courtesy of the Clatsop County Historical Society, Astoria, Oregon, Photo #3-930.* Below: *Rebuilding Commercial Street. After the blaze, Astoria was again constructed on wooden pilings, leaving it vulnerable to future fires—a fateful mistake. Courtesy Ray Hakala.*

ping. The accused man eyed the rope suspended menacingly over a tree limb, and glanced at the freshly dug grave waiting nearby. He wisely chose the whipping. He was later placed aboard a boat to Portland.

The following day the committee apprehended another man openly defying the vigilance committee. He was also arrested, found guilty, and given a choice of punishments. The rope and grave convinced him to also accept the whipping. He was dispatched on the morning boat.

As news of the second whipping spread throughout the town, stolen items began to mysteriously appear until the "city hall and fire engine room were so full of goods that the engine had to be taken out and kept on the streets to make room for the stolen goods." (25)

The town's sawmills were kept busy during the rebuilding of Astoria, producing lumber for buildings and streets. Astoria was again constructed on pilings, leaving it vulnerable to future fires—a fateful mistake.

Getting Around

The earliest settlers found it difficult to travel throughout Clatsop County. As late as 1855, there were no roads between Clatsop Plains and Astoria. Water transportation was widely used, and inhabitants traveled the well-worn Indian trails, but most communities remained isolated from each other for many years.

The opening of county roads initiated this comment by the editor of *The Weekly Astorian* on April 11, 1879: "It looks good to see a wagon and team on the streets of Astoria from the county. Such scenes have never until the last few months been witnessed." The completion in 1878 of the scow bay bridge connecting Lower Astoria and Uppertown was also a huge improvement. And in 1888, a road was built from Seaside to Young's Bay, a distance of fifteen miles.

Prior to 1888, a fleet of stagecoaches, which operated between the post office and Uppertown, provided public transportation throughout the city of Astoria. In May 1888, the Astoria Street Railway Company began a horse-drawn, four-wheeled streetcar service near the foot of Eighteenth Street. The horses pulled the cars along the tracks of the city from five forty-five a.m. to eleven p.m. at a fare of five cents. (26) This fare remained unchanged for almost thirty-four years. (27)

Regular steamer service began running from Astoria to San Francisco in the 1870s. The rivalry between the companies offering this service brought about low freight and passenger rates so there was considerable travel between Oregon and California. Steamers routinely made the trip from Portland to Astoria during the day, and tied up at Astoria for the night. "Steamer day" brought considerable revenue to the town, and merchants looked forward to the steamers arrival—much like present-day Astoria anticipates the modern day cruise ships.

In April 1892, the electric trolley arrived in Astoria.

Astoria's Churches

The very first church in Astoria was built on land donated by James Welch in 1853. It stood at the northwest corner of Fifteenth and Franklin streets, and was known as the Methodist Episcopal. Astoria's first public school classes were held there. In 1882, a new church was built over the river near the southeast corner of Eleventh and Duane streets, where "mischievous children fished out of the windows during Sunday School." (28) The present Methodist church at Eleventh and Franklin streets was dedicated in 1917 and contains many pews from the original church.

The first Episcopal church was constructed in 1865 near the corner of Eighth and Commercial streets. The present Grace Episcopal Church on Franklin between Fifteenth and Sixteenth streets was built on land donated by Mrs. Susan Shively. Church services began in the new church on Easter in 1886. Subsequent roadwork completed in front of the church resulted in the entrance being below street level. The church was hoisted up in 1891, and an additional room was added underneath.

The first Catholic priest to visit the area was Father Modeste Demers. He arrived in 1840 and stayed for several weeks before returning to Fort Vancouver. However, a Catholic church would not be built in Astoria for another thirty-four years. Construction began in 1873 on Astoria's first Catholic church on land purchased, in part, by soldiers stationed at Fort Stevens. Completed the following year, it was located on Grand Avenue between Fourteenth and Fifteenth streets near the site of the present gymnasium of the former Star of the Sea School. To address the needs of an expanding parish community, construction of a new church at the corner of 15th and Grand commenced in 1902. St. Mary, Star of the Sea, was dedicated in May 1903 and is still in use today.

Astoria's Presbyterians attended church on Clatsop Plains until a building was erected in 1883 at the northeast corner of Ninth and Duane streets. As the congregation grew, so did their need for a larger place of worship. Construction of a new building coincided closely with the con-

Methodist church built over the river in 1882. Children reportedly fished from the windows during Sunday school. Courtesy Ray Hakala.

struction of the Catholic church. Built with money donated by Captain George Flavel, a new Presbyterian church was dedicated in December of 1903. It is located at Eleventh and Grand.

Constructed around 1885, one of the oldest church structures in Astoria is the Finnish Apostolic Lutheran Church located at Tenth and Irving streets.

Above: *1885 Finnish Apostolic Lutheran Church.* Below: *St. Mary, Star of the Sea, dedicated in 1903. Both are still in use today.*

Lutheran church in Uppertown, now a private residence. Courtesy of the Clatsop County Historical Society, Astoria, Oregon, Photo #5312-520.

Building the South Jetty

The entrance to the Columbia River continued to be unpredictable and troublesome for vessels crossing in or out. Ships often waited two or three weeks for the right conditions to cross the Columbia bar. To rectify this problem, Congress in July 1884 authorized $100,000 to construct a jetty extending from Fort Stevens to a point several miles south of Cape Disappointment. A jetty would direct the river flow, which would help maintain the channel depth and keep heavy ocean waves from affecting boats entering and leaving the Columbia.

In 1884 the U. S. Congress authorized $100,000 for the construction of a jetty to ease the difficulty of entering and leaving the Columbia. A short railroad was built to transport the jetty's giant boulders, some of which exceeded fifty tons. Courtesy U. S. Army Corps of Engineers.

A short railroad was built to transport the gigantic boulders needed to construct the jetty. With some boulders exceeding fifty tons, this was no small task. Work on the five-mile-long jetty began in 1885 and continued for the next ten years. When completed, it appeared to have the desired effect—an increased channel depth, but twelve years later, there was a noticeable decrease in the depth of the channel. An extension to the jetty began in 1903, taking another ten years to complete. At its completion, the South Jetty was about seven miles long, creating a channel depth of approximately thirty feet at low tide. The North Jetty in Washington was completed in 1917. By the time both jetties were finished, "approximately nine million tons of rock had been deposited in the river." (29)

The onslaught of waves continues to weaken the jetties. In 2005, the North Jetty was repaired with close to 58,000 tons of rock. Several holes were discovered in the top portion of the South Jetty, and large rocks had been washed away, leaving only the concrete base, making the end of the jetty a mile shorter than it was originally. Fearing the jetty might break down and allow sand to clog the shipping channel, a two-year project commenced in May 2006 to repair the century-old structure. The May 9, 2006, *Daily Astorian* reported that an estimated 145,000 tons of rock would be needed, with boulders averaging eleven- to seventeen-tons each. Unlike the initial jetty construction, each stone would need to be carefully fitted into place. Continued maintenance of the jetties is a priority, as a breach could potentially stop all shipping through the Columbia.

Dredging had routinely taken place along the Columbia River to maintain an authorized channel depth of forty feet. Today, the navigation channel is authorized to forty-three feet to accommodate the larger fleet of international bulk cargo and container ships.

Columbia River Lights

A lighthouse was constructed at Point Adams in 1875, but with the completion of the South Jetty, which literally pushed back the ocean, the lighthouse was rendered obsolete in 1899. It was replaced by a light-house constructed on Desdemona Sands, a dangerous sand bar inside the river's entrance. Its light stood thirty-five feet above the water and could be seen for a distance of one mile. The sands and the lighthouse were named after the American vessel *Desdemona*, which wrecked in the area in 1857. Although no longer standing, the light station's pilings are still visible at low tide, to the west of the Astoria Bridge.

In addition to lighthouses, ships were used to light the way into the river. Probably the most isolated and dangerous duty in the U.S. Light-house Service was aboard a lightship. The vessel remained in place no matter how fierce the gales, or how thick the fog, and was in constant danger of being rammed by other ships. Severe winter storms brought eighty- to ninety-knot winds and many crew members were seasick most of the time.

Above: *The* Columbia River No. 604, *the last lightship in service on the West Coast, is on display at the Columbia River Maritime Museum.* Below: *The* Columbia River No. 50 *was the first ship assigned to the Columbia River channel. Courtesy U. S. Coast Guard.*

The first lightship station on the Pacific Coast was located at the approach to the main channel of the Columbia River. The first ship assigned to that station was the *Columbia River No. 50*, a 112-foot sailing vessel built in San Francisco. The Lighthouse Board in 1867 began numbering its lightships as a means of keeping track of them. The *Columbia River No. 50* was placed into service on April 9, 1892. The ship's light was a set of oil lamps hoisted to the top of the mast, where they could be seen from all directions. The ship had no propulsion engine, and had to be towed to its station.

Columbia River No. 50 remained in service until November 1899, when the ship's two-inch mooring chain snapped during a gale, leaving the vessel to helplessly drift in seventy-four mph winds. After attempts to tow the ship failed, grounding the vessel seemed the only option. The ship was beached on a strip of sand off Cape Disappointment where it remained for over a year. A marine railway was later built at the site, and the ship was successfully hauled to Bakers Bay, Washington. Hull repairs were made and the ship was towed to Portland, where it was painstakingly repaired. *Columbia River No. 50* returned to its station in August 1901 where it remained until it was retired from duty in 1909.

The lightships continued to sit as beacons at the entrance of the Columbia River until 1979, when a large, forty-two-foot navigational buoy replaced them. The last lightship in service on the West Coast was the *Columbia River No. 604*, a 128-foot vessel that served for twenty-nine years. It is currently on display at the Columbia River Maritime Museum and is open for tours. The large buoy, which was eventually replaced by a smaller one, is also on display outside the museum.

Early Coast Guard

One of the first stations of the U. S. Life Saving Service in the Pacific Northwest was located at Cape Disappointment. This lifeboat station, established in 1877, was charged with assisting mariners in distress who were close to the beach. Most of these stations consisted of no more than seven men who spent long hours training with their rescue equipment. When a ship was visibly in danger, a crewman jumped into his small, shore-based boat equipped with nothing more than his brawn, and paddled frantically through the turbulent surf to offer assistance.

The man largely responsible for the development of the lifeboat station was Joel Munson who, from 1865 until 1877, tended the Cape

Life savers paddling through the surf to a wreck, circa 1900. Courtesy of the Clatsop County Historical Society, Astoria, Oregon, Photo #4674-348.

Disappointment Lighthouse. In March 1865, the bark *Industry* wrecked near the cape with twenty-four people on board. Only seven survived. Munson, distraught that more people could not be saved, recovered a battered lifeboat from the wreck on the beach. He proceeded to rebuild it for use as a lifesaving boat. Munson was an accomplished fiddler, so he funded his life saving project by organizing dances in Astoria. Through his efforts the life saving station was established at Cape Disappointment, and Munson's rebuilt lifeboat was included in the station's first equipment.

The Railroad

Astoria dreamed for years of securing a railroad line to Portland—the primary thing it needed to make Astoria the seaport of the Northwest. As early as 1853, surveys were made for a rail line connecting the city to the northern transcontinental route. But ultimately Astoria lost out, and the northern route terminated in Puget Sound, Washington.

The determined Astorians did not give up easily, and there were several failed attempts at constructing a rail line to Portland. One project, a southern route along the Young's and Nehalem rivers, ran out of money after miles of land had been graded and tunnel excavation under Saddle

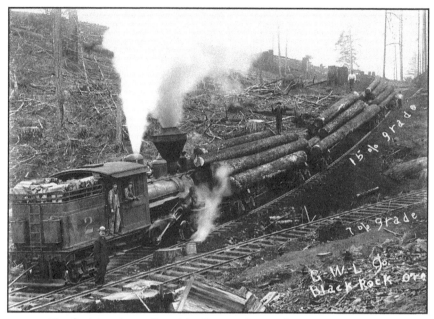

The first logging railroad in Clatsop County began operating in 1886. Eventually, the hills and valleys of the county were covered with a network of rails totaling hundreds of miles. Courtesy Salem Public Library Historic Photograph Collections.

Mountain had begun. Until 1895, the only line completed was from Young's Bay to Seaside, incorporated in 1890 as the Astoria & South Coast Railway.

Portland remained the goal, and Astoria persevered. Finally, in 1895, with the help of Andrew B. Hammond, the Astoria & Columbia River Railroad began construction of a fifty-mile rail line along the Columbia River that would connect with the Northern Pacific Railroad at the town of Goble (on the west bank of what is now Kalama, Washington). On May 16, 1898, the first train arrived in Astoria from Portland with seven hundred celebrating passengers. Astoria had its rail connection to Portland, making it no longer necessary to rely on river transportation.

The line later connected with the Astoria & South Coast Railway, creating a link from Portland to Seaside. For generations, vacationing families rode the train from Portland to Seaside's sandy beaches. A regularly advertised feature of the railroad was the "Daddy Trains," which brought working fathers back and forth on the weekends between Portland and the coast. At the peak of railway activity, eight passenger trains a day ran between Astoria, Seaside and Portland.

FIRST TRAIN TO PORTLAND
A&C R.R. MAY 16. 1858

On May 16, 1898, the first train arrived in Astoria from Portland, carrying seven hundred celebrating passengers. Courtesy of the Clatsop County Historical Society, Astoria, Oregon, Photo #4003-235.

Railroad construction in the Pacific Northwest had a significant impact on the developing ports of Portland, Tacoma and Seattle, making it easier to export wheat, lumber, and wool from the interior. Astoria's twenty-year delay in obtaining a railroad link to Portland sealed its fate. It would never attain the desired status of "seaport of the Northwest."

Improved Logging

The arrival of the railroad to Astoria gave a sizeable boost to the lumber industry. Besides creating a market in railroad ties, rail lines were used in logging operations. The first logging railroad in Clatsop County began operating in 1886, opening up areas previously inaccessible to oxen or horse teams. The hills and valleys of Clatsop County were eventually covered with a network of rails totaling hundreds of miles. During those days the only way to reach the logging camps was by railroad, so the workers lived at the camps. Eventually, logging railroads were abandoned in favor of log trucks. In 1941, the Crown Zellerbach Corporation discontinued its railroad operations in Clatsop County.

Technological advances also boosted the logging industry in the 1880s. The two-bladed (or double-bitted) axe and the crosscut saw were vital tools in those days. An axe with two blades allowed the logger to cut with a sharp axe for twice as long during the day. The crosscut saw had a handle on each end that enabled two men to work from opposite sides of a tree. Some saws were as long as fourteen feet, and even then were often not long enough to cut through the massive coastal trees.

The invention of steam donkey engines revolutionized log handling. Steam donkeys created steam that powered winches, enabling logs to be pulled in by cables. Consisting of a boiler and three steam-powered winches mounted on a skid, a steam donkey was operated by a "skin-ner," who worked the winches, and a "swamper," who kept the boiler going. Anchored to a tree by one of its cables, the donkey dragged itself along the forest floor by its own power. John Chitwood in about 1889 was the first logger in Clatsop County to use a steam donkey, which he adapted from a ship's steam winch. The steam-powered operations were efficient and could be used during the rainy winter months. One down-side to them was an increase in the accident rate among loggers, and the damage the engines caused to the forest. The steam donkey remained in use in the Coast Range until World War II, when the invention of gasoline- and diesel-powered machines rendered it obsolete.

Sawmills benefited from the invention in the 1880s of a mechanical-driven band saw, a new double circular saw, and mechanical blowers that sped up the disposal of sawdust from the mills. Lumber products became more sophisticated, finding markets in the East Coast, and in England, Europe, and South Africa.

In 1886, R. M. Brayne designed and built the first pulp mill in Oregon at Young's River Falls. Ocean steamers carried tons of ground wood pulp each week to a paper company in Stockton, California, where it was pro-cessed and made into paper. The Willamette Falls and Paper Company in Oregon City later purchased the mill, and the pulp was transported up the Columbia River for processing in Oregon City. The Young's River mill closed in 1904, and the machinery was moved to Oregon City.

John C. Trullinger, one of Astoria's most successful sawmill operators, introduced electricity to the city of Astoria. In 1885, Trullinger installed ten thirty-amp lights; eight at the sawmill, one in front of the *Daily Astorian*, and one between the mill and his home. They were first lit on Christmas Eve, powered by run-off waste from his sawmill. Trullinger upgraded his operation in 1890, adding a two thousand-lamp incan-

Steam donkeys revolutionized log handling. Anchored to a tree by one of its cables, the donkey dragged itself along the forest floor by its own power. Photograph, circa 1909. Courtesy of the Clatsop County Historical Society, Astoria, Oregon, Photo #6258-600.

descent generator. He continued to expand and upgrade his electrical system until it was purchased by the Astoria Electric Company in 1902.

Ellis Island of the Columbia

The completion of the transcontinental railroad and the discovery of Oregon's lush forests for harvesting timber created a population boom in the region. Many newcomers arrived by ship, so the U.S. government purchased an abandoned cannery at Knappton Cove on the north shore of the Columbia River for use as a quarantine station. To protect its citizens from diseases like bubonic plague, yellow fever and small pox, Congress in 1891 passed a law requiring the medical inspection of all arriving immigrants. Health stations were established at ports of entry into the United States. New York's Ellis Island opened in 1892, and the Columbia River Quarantine Station began operating seven years later. It was one of four major points of entry on the West Coast, serving 133 ships and processing 6,120 individuals during its first year of operation.

All ships entering the Columbia were boarded and inspected, and if fumigation or quarantine were warranted, they anchored at Knappton Cove. Fumigation consisted of sealing the ship and boiling cauldrons of sulfur. The sulfur fumes killed the rats and fleas that caused disease.

Upon arriving, male and female immigrants disrobed and showered in separate bathrooms on the pier, while their clothing went through a delousing process. They were then inspected for disease. If any passengers or crew were found to be ill, the entire ship would be quarantined. The December 11, 1900 *Astoria Evening Budget* described the procedure the passengers endured:

> *. . . they pass into a room where they are relieved of their clothes, then pass on into the baths, all shower, of which there are several. From the baths they pass on into another room where they are furnished clean or new clothing, and from which they may be let out on either side of the wharf. . . There is no going backwards. After taking the bath the passenger does not go where he was before the bath. . . If it is thought necessary to detain the passengers, they are then kept for about 14 days.*

The quarantine station hospital, built in 1912, had two wards that could accommodate eight to ten beds. At the end of both wards were two small isolation wards with their own entries.

In *The Sunday Oregonian* on October 2, 1921, the station was praised for "its ability to make certain that incoming aliens are clean and fit to mingle with healthy humans and that danger of transferring disease from foreign countries is eliminated." This statement may have been influenced by the flu epidemic sweeping the globe from 1918 to 1920. Historian Liisa Penner estimates that 164 people died from influenza-related causes in Clatsop County from October 1918 to January 1919.

The quarantine station was originally administered in Astoria by the U.S. Marine Hospital Services and, later, the U.S. Public Health Service. Doctors working at the station were ferried back and forth from Astoria. The quarantine office was relocated to Portland in 1928, and the facility permanently closed ten years later.

There is a privately owned museum in the former hospital building, and the "dolphin" docking posts where the ships moored are still standing and in good condition. Knappton Cove Quarantine Station is located in Washington, three miles east of the Astoria Bridge, and is listed on the National Register of Historic Places.

Above: *Ellis Island of the Columbia. Old quarantine station hospital at Knappton Cove, built in 1912.* Below: *Knappton port, early 1900s. Courtesy Salem Public Library Historic Photographs Collection.*

The Strike of 1896

1896 was a critical year for the Lower Columbia salmon industry. Even though the prior year brought a record number of salmon, canneries began to struggle with escalating operating costs, rising fish prices, and competition with the growing canning industry in Alaska. To top it off, gillnet fishermen were at odds with fish trappers, most of whom set their traps near the mouth of the river in Bakers Bay, Washington. The canneries, to ensure a steady supply of cheap fish, owned many of these traps.

Hoping to resurrect the Columbia chinook as the leading brand of salmon in the world, the canneries united, and in April they formed the Columbia River Packers Association. To successfully compete in the world market, they decided to pay fishermen one cent less per pound in order to lower the price of the finished product. Outraged to learn the price for chinook salmon would be lowered to four cents per pound, the fishermen's union insisted on five cents—and neither side would budge.

On April 10, gillnet fishermen voted to strike, declaring that no one would be allowed to fish on the river. Undaunted, the canneries continued their fish trap operations. Tempers flared, and an emissary of angry men from the Fishermen's Protective Union destroyed trap-fishing equipment in Baker's Bay. The fish trap operators appealed to the government for protection, and Washington's Governor McGraw dispatched soldiers to the beaches near Ilwaco and Chinook, Washington.

Six weeks into the strike, the violence escalated when two men were shot while fishing on the river—one was hit in the forehead, dying instantly, and the other was wounded but survived. Still, the canneries and the fishermen could not reach an agreement.

Local businessmen were agitated because the strike was having an adverse affect on the local economy. Articles appeared in the *Astorian* stressing the need for diversity in the market—that Astoria should attract industries not dependent on fishing. Fishermen began to leave en masse. It looked like there would not be a fishing season on the Lower Columbia in 1896. Fishermen who remained threatened businessmen with bodily harm or burned property unless they supported the fishermen's position.

Violence struck again. During the early evening hours of May 28, a woman and three men were murdered while boating on the river near Clifton. Clearly, something had to be done. On June 16, the steamer *Harvest Queen* arrived in Astoria with almost five hundred members of

Above: *The Union Fishermen's Cooperative Packing Company was Astoria's largest cannery in the early 1900s* (note: photo mislabeled). *Courtesy of the Clatsop County Historical Society, Astoria, Oregon, Photo #7048-330.* Below: *The upscale Cannery Pier Hotel was built on the site of the former cannery. Courtesy Cannery Pier Hotel.*

Astoria from Uppertown, looking out the mouth of the Columbia River, circa 1914.

the Oregon National Guard. The guard descended on the town, setting up quarters at the courthouse and surrounding grounds. Their extensive arsenal included two twelve-pound cannons and two Gatling guns. Two days later the guard moved its headquarters to the custom house.

With the National Guard's arrival, the threat of violence diminished, and canneries began receiving an abundance of fish. But union fishermen held firm in their demands for five cents per pound, even as the first load of salmon was shipped east. Finally, after a union meeting on June 20, the fishermen voted to end the strike, agreeing to accept four and one-half cents per pound. The strike had lasted almost two and a half months. The National Guard left Astoria on June 24.

The fishermen, disgruntled at having lost the battle, decided to pool their resources and build a cannery of their own. Two hundred men of primarily Finnish descent established the Union Fishermen's Cooperative Packing Company, and by 1904 it was the largest cannery in Astoria. The Finnish immigrants were brought up amidst the cooperative movement in Western Europe, so they designed their new company with the same structure—fishermen were not paid by the number of fish they caught, but rather they received a share of the company's profits. The Cooperative remained a fishermen-owned business until the late 1940s. The cannery was located between the west mooring basin and the Astoria Bridge. The site of the cannery is now home to the Cannery Pier Hotel. Completed in 2005, the forty-six-room upscale hotel has a remarkable resemblance to the old cannery.

Woman Surgeon

Dr. Bethenia Owens-Adair was a notable figure in Oregon in the late 1800s, and is thought to be Oregon's first woman surgeon. Throughout

Library of Congress PAN US GEOG-Oregon no. 38.

her career Owens-Adair was committed to the women's suffragist movement and to the Women's Christian Temperance Union. She advocated "the necessity of educating our children, through our public schools, as to the effects of alcohol and narcotics on the human system." (30)

Bethenia Angelina Owens was born in 1840 in Missouri, the second of nine children, making the overland journey to Oregon with her family in 1843. They settled on Clatsop Plains. At fourteen, and barely able to read or write, she married Legrand Hill. After four years in an abusive marriage, she gathered up her two-year-old son, George, and moved into her father's house. The following year she sued for divorce and the restoration of her maiden name.

Owens attended school alongside her son, while supporting them both by any means available—washing, ironing, berry-picking, and housekeeping. She excelled so well in her studies that she and George lived for a time with her sister, Mrs. John Hobson, and Owens taught school at the Presbyterian Church on Clatsop Plains, recalling:

Of my sixteen pupils, there were three who were more advanced than myself, but I took their books home with me nights, and, with the help of my brother-in-law, I managed to prepare the lessons beforehand, and they never suspected my incompetency. (31)

It was during this time that Owens and her brother-in-law created the mammoth round of cheese as a fundraiser for the Sanitary Commission during the Civil War. (See *The Big Cheese*, Chapter 4).

Owens continued to find success teaching school, managing to save enough money to own a home of her own. She purchased a half lot in Astoria, and hired a carpenter to build "a small, three-roomed cottage, with a cosy [sic] little porch." (32)

While visiting family in Roseburg, she was persuaded to enter the business of dressmaking and millinery. She rented out her house in Astoria, and realized great profits in her new trade. By 1870, she had saved enough money to send her son to the University of California at Berkeley.

With her son safely off to college, Owens' lifelong fondness for nursing prompted her to seek out medical studies. Amid sneers and jeers from both family and friends, Owens enrolled in Philadelphia's Eclectic School of Medicine where she received her degree. Still thirsting for knowledge, she later enrolled in the University of Michigan, receiving a full medical degree in 1880. Years later, in 1899, Owens received a post-graduate degree from the Chicago Clinical School. Her son, George Hill, received his medical degree from Willamette University at the age of twenty-one.

In 1884, Owens met and married an old childhood friend, John Adair, Jr. (son of the first commissioned customs collector on the Pacific coast), and they took up residence near Astoria. However, this marriage also ended in divorce. Owens-Adair retired from her medical practice in 1905, but continued her work as a social and political activist.

One of Dr. Owens-Adair's strong beliefs was that insanity and criminal behavior were hereditary. She was very much in favor of the sterilization of the criminally insane and mentally retarded. Her work on the subject, *Human Sterilization: Its Social and Legislative Aspects* (1922), brought her recognition in the field.

In 1925, a sterilization statute was adopted as state law in Oregon, and the Board of Social Protection was formed. Oregon was one of thirty-three states to enact laws to provide forced sterilization, and over twenty-six hundred Oregonians underwent sterilizations during the sixty years in which the practice was permitted. (33) This state policy ended in 1983 with the abolishment of the Board of Social Protection.

Bethenia Owens-Adair died in 1926 at the age of eighty-six, just three days after attending the opening of the Astoria Column.

Prohibition

In the final years of the 1800s, the temperance movement gained momentum. Led by the Women's Christian Temperance Union (WCTU) and the Anti-Saloon League, public demonstrations against saloons were commonplace. Prohibition supporters envisioned a society with less crime and domestic abuse—a society where citizens, free from the debilitating effects of alcohol, would become stronger and more productive.

Dr. Bethenia Owens-Adair, thought to be Oregon's first female surgeon, was committed to the suffragist and temperance movements. Courtesy of the Clatsop County Historical Society, Astoria, Oregon, Photo #5595-00A.

Liquor control in Oregon had been a prominent issue for decades and, in fact, as early as 1844, Oregon's provisional government enacted a prohibition law that prevented the sale and distillation of "ardent spirits" in Oregon. It was repealed in 1849 by the territorial legislature.

In Astoria, W. W. Parker helped organize the first temperance society in Clatsop County. He worked diligently as a representative to the legislature for passage of a temperance bill. Mrs. Parker was secretary of the local WCTU of Astoria in 1885 when Dr. Owens-Adair was invited to speak on the necessity of teaching the evils of alcohol to public school children.

Wine-O label, Astoria Soda Works, 1918. During the Prohibition years those with good imaginations marketed non-alcoholic drinks with names associated with liquor. Courtesy Oregon State Archives, Trademark #1891.

The Finnish Temperance Society organized about 1887 and built a meeting hall in Uniontown. Suomi Hall was later sold to the Finnish Brotherhood, and is still used for their meetings today.

In November 1887, Oregon voters defeated a proposed amendment to the state constitution that would institute statewide prohibition. But the fight was far from over. In 1914, Oregon successfully passed legislation banning the manufacture and sale of alcoholic beverages.

During the prohibition years, those with good imaginations formulated non-alcoholic drinks with names associated with liquor. For instance, the Astoria Soda Works advertised "Wine-O: Made with fruit and berry juices—No artificial flavor used—Not carbonated." And for those who were willing to break the law, there was always the illegal still.

In 1933, voters repealed Oregon's constitutional prohibition amendment and, soon after, Oregon ratified the Twenty-first Amendment to the U.S. Constitution, repealing national prohibition.

Women's Rights

The National Woman Suffrage Association and the American Woman Suffrage Association were formed in 1869. By 1872, the suffrage movement was in full swing in Oregon, with Abigail Scott Duniway at the helm. County by county organizations eventually formed

Oregonians marched in the first national suffrage parade in Washington, D. C. Courtesy Library of Congress, Manuscript Division, Women of Protest: Photographs from the Records of the National Woman's Party [mnwp 159007].

into the Oregon Suffrage Association, and Oregonians marched in the first national suffrage parade in Washington, D. C. The first chairman of the Clatsop County chapter was Mrs. J. C. Trullinger, who remained in that position throughout the 1880s, until her daughter, Belle, took over the chairmanship. Belle later became First Lady of Oregon as wife of Governor Theodore T. Geer.

Curiously, Astoria was ahead of most places when it came to women's rights, as is evident in an advertisement for Astoria's schools on January 15, 1884:

Besides the prestige of having the finest public school building North of San Francisco, Astoria public schools have the distinction of being taught exclusively by women. There are ten teachers employed in the three schools and their salaries are considerably above the average pay of teachers in this state. In this, Astoria recognizes the principle that if a woman can fill any department of industry as well as a man she is entitled to the same wages a man would be paid for the same work. (34)

For some time, the equal suffrage movement joined the temperance movement in an attempt to enact both social reforms. However, the two movements had trouble dividing their focus between the two issues. In Oregon, Abigail Scott Duniway blamed the prohibitionists for many of the suffragist's defeats at the polls. By 1912, when Oregon voters enacted women's suffrage into law, the two movements had essentially split.

Hopes & Shattered Dreams
1900-1922

Astoria, circa 1905. Courtesy of the Clatsop County Historical Society, Astoria, Oregon, Photo #428-900.

Astoria and the mouth of the Columbia River, circa 1915.

Still Growing

Astoria greeted the new century as the second largest city in Oregon, boasting a population of almost nine thousand. Astoria's school district had six grammar schools and a high school that accommodated about fifteen hundred children and thirty-one teachers. (1) Astoria City Hall was constructed in 1904 at the corner of Sixteenth and Exchange, the site of the original 1811 Astor Company burial ground. Currently, the building is occupied by the Heritage Museum. In 1939, City Hall was relocated to a cast-off bank building at the corner of Eleventh and Duane, where it remains to this day. The old wooden courthouse was replaced in 1908 with a new one built of stone. Construction began in 1904, but due to financial and contractual issues, it took four years to build. That courthouse is still in use at Eighth and Commercial streets.

The April 2, 1911, *Morning Astorian*, ran an advertisement for a new residential area called Hanthorn's Addition, declaring "Astoria has a population of 14,000," and "investors all over the country are looking to Astoria and there is no place anywhere that offers better opportunities."

The Centennial Year

Astoria in 1911 celebrated the arrival one hundred years earlier of the first European-Americans to set foot there. Advertising for the event ran in the *San Francisco Call*, the *Los Angeles Times*, the *Seattle Post Intelligencer*, and *The Oregonian*. In the *Morning Astorian* on March 23, there was an announcement of special round trip train fares ranging from seventy- to eighty-five dollars from "great centres of the country."

Sprucing up the town for the big event was on everyone's minds. In

Library of Congress, PAN US GEOG-Oregon no. 34.

addition, the editor of the *Morning Astorian* recognized the potential fire danger on Commercial Street, addressing the topic on March 23:

> *The best interests of the Centennial forbid the further building of cheap temporary structures upon Commercial Street. . .or remodeling of the inflammable buildings which line it from end to end.*

The Centennial Committee and the Park Commission planned to erect a steel tower and observatory on Coxcomb Hill to commemorate the centennial. They also planned to build a highway leading to the site. But whether for lack of funds or lack of time to carry out such grandiose plans, the committee settled on a large ten-foot by fifty-foot sign with the wooden numerals 1811—1911. The sign was illuminated at night by incandescent light bulbs with electricity provided by the Hammond Lumber Company. Instead of a modern highway, a walking trail was slashed through the underbrush up the southwest slope of the hill.

The centennial celebration ran from August 10 to September 9, and the official colors were blue, white, and the American flag. An electric button pressed by President Taft in Washington, D.C. triggered a gong that launched the festivities. Oregon's Governor Oswald West and a presidential aide, John Barnett, presided over the celebrations. Ten thousand spectators packed Centennial Park (present-day Shively Park) to witness the speeches and events. American Indians, including representatives from the Nez Perce and Yakama tribes, were invited, despite the irony of being the very people who were displaced from their homelands as a result of the westward expansion.

The president of the Centennial Committee was the mayor, Dr. H.

*Representatives from Nez Perce and Yakama tribes
at Astoria's 1911 centennial.*

L. Henderson. Henderson was an eccentric individual who took great
pride in his appearance; that is, he left certain things to nature, and
shied away from shaving. During the centennial celebrations he reportedly offered free transportation to anyone whose whiskers were bigger
than his. "The *Sunday Oregonian* of August 27, 1911, said that the may-
or's whiskers were Astoria's attraction. Dr. Henderson's whiskers were
24 inches wide by 36 inches long and three inches thick. . . said to be the
largest whiskers on the Pacific Coast." (2)

Astorians not only planned a grand centennial celebration, they also
began looking favorably to the opening in 1914 of the Panama Canal,
as is evident in this editorial in the March 14, 1911, *Morning Astorian*:

> *The four years elapsing between the Astoria Centennial Jubilee and
> the opening of the Panama Canal are to be the vital preparatory,
> compensating years of this city. . . Never will she have another
> chance to get on her commercial feet and ensure her destiny among
> the Pacific ports. The work must be begun in this good year of 1911
> and continued faithfully and eagerly to put this place in line for the
> benefits to accrue from the opening of the great ditch.*

And a housing advertisement on April 2 stated that Astoria "is a

*Courtesy Library of Congress, Prints and
Photographs Division, [LC-US262-51285 DLC].*

flourishing city today and mark well with the opening of the Panama Canal will take a front place with San Francisco and Seattle as a commercial centre on the Pacific coast."

Astorians moved forward with their plans to turn Astoria into one of the foremost port cities of the Pacific by developing the port of Astoria. The port opened in 1914, the same year as the canal. But Astoria was not destined to take a "front place with San Francisco and Seattle." Initially there was an increase in maritime shipping when water freight became cheaper than rail freight, but Astoria ultimately did not benefit as it had so hoped. Most cargoes bypassed Astoria and were shipped directly to and from Portland.

Socialism in Astoria

During the nineteenth century a significant number of Finns arrived in the United States, many fleeing the anti-Finnish policies of the Russian government. At the turn of the twentieth century, Finnish immigration exploded. With the successful salmon canneries along the Columbia River, Finnish immigrants, many of whom were successful fishermen in Finland, jumped at the opportunity to make a reasonable living. After achieving success, they encouraged their relatives in Finland to join them. This plea resulted in a large number of Finnish

The entrance to Centennial Park, currently known as Shively Park, circa 1911. Courtesy of the Clatsop County Historical Society, Astoria, Oregon, Photo #14,786-111-5.

men making the trip to Astoria. The 1880 county census reported 203 Finns, with only fourteen of them women. Of the 189 males listed, 171 were identified as fishermen. By 1900, there were more Finns in Astoria than any other nationality. By the start of the First World War, more than 200,000 Finns had arrived in the United States.

After the fishermen's strike in 1896, Finnish fishermen began taking an interest in the labor movement. In 1904, the Astoria Socialist Club formed with twenty-seven members, instituting evening programs for the purpose of educating the public in socialism. In a few years, its membership numbered between three and four hundred. In 1911, they constructed a meeting hall that became the hub of social activity in Uniontown. They organized a choir, a theater group, orchestra, sports club, sewing club, and a speakers' bureau for the purpose of spreading socialist ideals. They even set up their own shops to sell clothing and tobacco so members would not have to patronize businesses hostile to labor organizations. Until the hall burned down in 1923, it was the hub of cultural life for Astoria's socialist Finns. The club also founded a socialist newspaper, *Toveri* ("comrade"), which became one of three major newspapers of the national Finnish Socialist Federation.

As socialists from Finland continued to arrive, socialism perpetu-

The Astoria Socialist Club's meeting hall, built in 1911, was the hub of cultural life for Astoria's socialist Finns. Another group, the Church Finns, espoused more conservative views. Courtesy Ray Hakala.

ated among Finnish-Americans. However, not all of Astoria's Finns espoused the socialist view, which created a split in the Finnish community—the Socialist Finns and the Church Finns (with conservative views). Another split occurred following the Russian Revolution of 1917 and World War I, when the communist movement began to take root and a majority of those in the Finnish Socialist Federation supported communist ideals. During the Russian Revolution, Finland itself was in the midst of a civil war—between the "Reds" (Communists) and the "Whites" (Social Democratics). As more Finns emigrated to Astoria, many brought with them communist sympathies.

Many Finnish immigrants, dissatisfied at not finding the classless society they had hoped, planned to design their own community. Thinking the best place for such a society to be a remote fishing village in northern Russia, more than fifty Finns left Astoria in the 1920s and 1930s in pursuit of this dream. Too late they discovered the harsh realities of the Soviet Union. Very few were lucky enough to make it back to the United States. Most were never heard from again.

Modern Transportation

In 1904, the first automobile arrived in Clatsop County. Called the Orient Motor Buckboard, it was a favorite car in the area because it could easily tackle the muddy county roads. Astoria's first car dealer was located on Bond Street. Reliance Electrical Works advertised the Buckboard as "the most practical machine for hill climbing and rough roads. Ten inch road clearance." (3)

Railroad construction enticed new immigrants to the Northwest, offering them a faster and more comfortable cross-country journey. The improved rail line followed the north side of the Columbia River Gorge, switching to the south shore at Vancouver for the final leg to Astoria. Tourists made regular train trips to the beach along the scenic river, and in 1905 it cost four dollars for the weekend round trip from Portland. (4) But the train had its share of problems and during the wet winter months would sometimes arrive several hours late. When the stretch of new highway was completed in 1915 between Astoria and Portland, creating a shorter trip by automobile, train travel gradually began to lose its appeal. Even so, a beautiful brick train depot was constructed in Astoria in 1924 to accommodate the arriving visitors. In 1926, the Roosevelt Coast Military Highway was completed, making it possible to drive from Astoria all the way to California. In 1931, the road was

Ferry crossings of the Columbia River began in 1921. After the attack on Pearl Harbor, Tourist No. 2 *(pictured here) was commandeered and used to lay flotation mines in the river. Courtesy Oregon Department of Transportation.*

re-named the Oregon Coast Highway.

In 1952, passenger train service in the county was discontinued. In 1958, freight service came to an end. The Seaside line was abandoned in 1978, and by the late 1980s, all track west of Astoria had been removed.

In 1921, a fifteen-car ferry began making regular crossings of the Columbia River from Astoria's Fourteenth Street pier. The sixty-four-foot boat, called *The Tourist*, was built by the Wilson Shipbuilding Company of Astoria, and was owned and operated by Captain Fritz Elfving. The following year, he reportedly carried 6,500 vehicles and 25,600 people across the river between June 15 and September 10. (5) He later built a second and third ferry, *Tourist No. 2* and *Tourist No. 3*. After the attack on Pearl Harbor in 1941, *Tourist No. 2* was commandeered and used to lay mines in the river. (See *Second World War* in Chapter 6.)

The State of Oregon purchased Captain Elfving's company in 1946, assigning its operation to the State Highway Department. Ferry service continued until the completion of the Astoria Bridge in 1966. Today the Fourteenth Street ferry dock includes interpretive displays. A radio speaker allows visitors to hear live conversations of river pilots and the Coast Guard as they go about their work on the river.

Declining Salmon

Astoria during the nineteenth century was the largest salmon producer in the world. But after decades of enormous fish runs, the early twentieth century arrived amid concerns for fish conservation. Of particular concern was the prized chinook salmon. Declining salmon runs resulted in a progressively shorter season on the Columbia River, so cannery owners attempted to can a variety of other products, including beef, crab and shrimp, but none proved successful. Canneries gradually began to close or to merge with one another, and by 1903, only seven canneries remained. As the decline of the spring chinook became evident, the remaining canneries shifted their harvest to the fall chinook, which were considered inferior.

In response to the disappearing salmon, the industry banned certain fishing methods. Fish wheels were banned in Oregon in 1927. However, not enough funds were allocated to police the river, so these restrictions were seldom enforced.

Many fish wheel owners evaded the ban by simply moving their gear to the Washington shore. In 1935, fish wheels, along with stationary nets and seines, were prohibited in Washington. Seines were outlawed in Oregon in 1949. But even as some forms of fishing were being restricted, other fishing methods emerged. Gasoline engines arrived on the Columbia in 1898. By 1906 half of the boats operating from Astoria had gasoline-powered engines.

Salmon trolling began in 1912 off the mouth of the Columbia. From 1921 through 1958, an average of fifteen million pounds of chinook salmon was harvested in the Columbia, down from an average catch of twenty-five million pounds from 1889 to 1920. (6)

Logging

Fishing may have slackened in the early 1900s, but the Northwest lumber industry initially prospered. Around the turn of the century lumbermen began migrating from the Midwest where the forests were

Horse seines were eventually prohibited on the Columbia in response to a decline in salmon. Courtesy of the Clatsop County Historical Society, Astoria, Oregon, Photo #7344-310.

decimated by over-logging. These men were lured to the Northwest by rising lumber prices. In 1902 there were approximately 133 lumber camps operating on the Lower Columbia River and its tributaries. Clatsop County was Oregon's number one lumber producer in 1920, with the Hammond Mill handling 450,000 board feet a day. (7) In 1929, lumber production in the Northwest was at an all-time high, making up one-half the value of regional exports. (8)

It is estimated that in the early 1900s the Hammond Mill in Astoria employed about six hundred people of different nationalities. Besides Italian, Greek, Japanese and Middle Eastern workers, there were nearly one hundred East Indians living in bunkhouses along the waterfront near the mill in Alderbrook. Beginning in about 1906, until the mill burned on September 11, 1922, Birch Street between Fifty-first and Fifty-second streets was Astoria's so-called "Hindu Alley."

First World War

World War I affected the Pacific Northwest in a variety of ways. The Oregon economy thrived with the production of war materials and ships, and wheat and lumber prices soared. The lumber trade expanded, with most logging taking place in the coastal mountains where Sitka spruce was harvested for use in airplane construction. 1918 saw the completion of a three hundred-foot-wide, thirty-foot-deep Columbia River navigation channel. As a result, oceangoing cargo more than tripled in the next ten years.

At the onset of the war and to celebrate Independence Day 1917, an enormous flagpole—a gnarled two hundred-year-old spruce—was erected on Coxcomb Hill. The finishing touch was an eighty-pound bronze ball that sat on top. On the Fourth of July, as a gigantic flag ascended the pole, a band played "America" and "The Star Spangled Banner," and cheers could be heard from the hundreds of people watching from downtown. The flagpole remained atop the hill for the next six years, until it was struck by lightning during a severe thunderstorm.

Fort Stevens took on new life since its construction during the Civil War as troops drilled and trained on its parade grounds. In Astoria, the war boosted the declining salmon fishing and canning industry when the United States government began buying nearly every can of salmon. The demand for ships created a major ship building industry in the Pacific Northwest, and four large shipyards emerged in Astoria: McEachern in Young's Bay; Wilson at Smith Point; Rodgers at Pier Two; and Leathers on the Columbia River. A belt line railroad was constructed around Smith Point to serve the yards, but the shipbuilding industry was short lived. With the armistice, the last ship was launched in June 1919. The river pilings that supported the railroad are still visible in the bay along West Marine Drive.

When the war began, Astoria's citizens, led by Mayor Francis Clay Harley, lobbied for a naval base at Tongue Point. It took several years, but Congress finally approved the construction of an Astoria submarine and destroyer base, with one stipulation—Astoria was required to donate the land to the government. In 1921, after the passage of a bond to purchase Tongue Point from A. B. Hammond for $100,000, (9) Clatsop County transferred ownership of 395 acres to the federal government. Dredging began the same year and, by 1924, a breakwater and four wooden piers had been constructed. But the base was

Constructed during the Civil War, Fort Stevens took on new life in World War I. Courtesy of the Clatsop County Historical Society, Astoria, Oregon, Photo #5043-751.

never used. With decreased military appropriations following the war, the base was ultimately abandoned. Repeated requests that the Navy return the property to the city of Astoria went unanswered. The site was used as a community picnic ground until 1939. (See Chapter 6, *Second World War*)

The Oregon economy collapsed immediately after the war, beginning with the cancellation of shipbuilding and lumber orders. As hordes of unemployed searched for work, more than 50,000 people left Oregon. (10) Astoria's population peaked in 1920, with 14,027 residents. Ten years later, the census revealed that 4,000 people had left Astoria.

Ku Klux Klan

Paranoia swept the country following World War I, and Oregon was not exempt. A general fear of anarchists, communists and immigrants triggered some citizens to react violently. Many communities, concerned about social immorality and lawlessness, yearned to return to the ideals of the Victorian era where character, home, and family prevailed—just the sort of atmosphere in which the Ku Klux Klan thrived. Klan membership in the West was comprised mostly of poor, rural and fundamentalist Protestants who believed that evil prevailed in the cities. But it also attracted the support of many middle class Americans by promoting improved law enforcement, honest government, better public schools, and traditional family life.

Prohibition had come to the Pacific Northwest in 1914 and, by the 1920s, Astoria was rife with prohibition violations, including gambling, prostitution, and political corruption. Liquor violations were common in area roadhouses and speakeasies. Catholics and Protestants were in agreement that vice in Astoria was out of control, so together they formed the Astoria Law Enforcement League to aid local law enforcement in catching offenders. This unity against immorality and political corruption paved the way for the Ku Klux Klan's entrance into Astoria. In 1921, Lem Dever, editor of the Oregon Klan's periodical *Western American*, arrived to lead the Astoria Klan.

In 1920, Oregon's population was eighty-five percent white and native born, and ninety percent Protestant. (11) The Ku Klux Klan typically thrived in areas with high native white populations. And although Astoria had the highest immigrant population in the state, the majority of its immigrants were white Protestants, which the Klan wasted no time in uniting.

One way they accomplished this was through racial and religious tension. The Astoria Klan circulated pamphlets alleging false claims against the Catholic Church—in particular, against the Knights of Columbus. At the same time, Klan members visited Protestant churches, making generous donations in the process. Many Protestants were impressed with the Klan members, believing them to be defenders of moral and social reform. Consequently, Astoria Klan membership grew. The July 2, 1922, *Morning Astorian*, reported that 250 men joined the Klan.

The Ku Klux Klan wielded considerable power in the state legislature, and their influence was evident in the elections of 1922. In Astoria, the Klan ticket won the majority of votes, electing the mayor and four city commissioners. The Klan also successfully organized a recall of the county sheriff.

The Oregon Klan actively supported the election of Governor Walter Pierce, whose endorsement of the anti-Catholic Compulsory Education Act fit well with the Klan's persecution of immigrants and Catholics. Adopted in November 1922, the Act required all children between

Following World War I, the Klan's influence grew in the Northwest. At its peak more than two thousand Astorians, including five ministers, were members. Photograph, circa 1920. Courtesy of the Clatsop County Historical Society, Astoria, Oregon, Photo #3503-540.

the ages of eight and sixteen to attend public schools. Although voters approved the measure, the U.S. Supreme Court in 1925 ruled the Compulsory Education Act unconstitutional.

Astoria passed a new city charter during the primary elections of 1922 in which the municipal government was changed to a managerial form of governance. Under the new charter, a common council composed of the mayor and the four Klan-endorsed commissioners selected a city manager who would appoint all other city officials. This change was a significant factor in the eventual decline of the Klan in Astoria.

When the new mayor and commissioners took office following the devastating fire of 1922, they began reconstruction efforts. But when the new city manager acted contrary to Klan wishes and began appointing officials of his own choosing, the Klan initiated a recall petition. However, the community was pleased with the way the city was handling the rebuilding of Astoria and had no interest in a recall. The Klan did not fade away quietly. The October 15, 1925, *Astoria Evening Budget*: "A fiery cross 35 feet high flared from the top of Coxcomb Hill last night."

In the years prior to the Klan's final demise in 1928, more than 2,000 Astorians, including five ministers, had been members of the Ku Klux Klan. (12) In fact, Clatsop County had the second highest Klan membership in the state after Portland.

Fire of 1922

In the early hours of December 8, 1922, Astoria's business district burned to the ground. No one knows how the fire started, but of the many theories, the most credible is that it started in the basement of a restaurant at Twelfth and Commercial streets, where packing material had been tossed too close to the pilot light of a water heater.

Most downtown buildings sat on wood pilings over the river, including the wooden streets connecting them, just as they had been before the destructive fire of 1883. The blaze raced quickly through the city made of wood, and it seemed there was nothing anyone could do about it. Power went off, gas mains exploded, business owners frantically

Only the columns of the magnificent Weinhard-Astoria Hotel were left standing after the fire. They were later placed in Shively Park. Courtesy of the Clatsop County Historical Society, Astoria, Oregon, Photo #11,129-935.

Above: *Once again, Astoria's business district burned to the ground.* Below: *When the 1922 inferno finally burned out, thirty-two city blocks were destroyed and over two hundred shops, hotels, and businesses were in ruins. Shaded area indicates extent of damage. Photo [#11,116-935] and map courtesy of the Clatsop County Historical Society, Astoria, Oregon.*

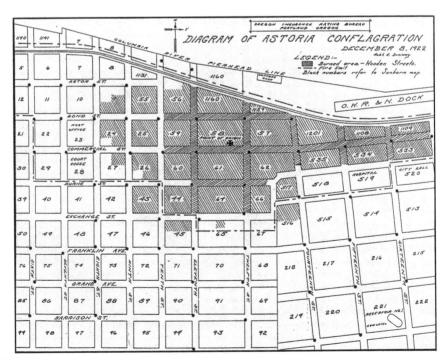

tried to salvage goods from their stores, and looters swooped in to take advantage. Although Astoria was equipped with fire hydrants, the water mains were located beneath the wooden roadways. The burning streets collapsed, taking the water pipes and hydrants with them.

In a last ditch effort to contain the blaze, townspeople resorted to using dynamite. Homes and businesses were blown up all around the burning town in an effort to create a firebreak. Sherman Lovell described saving his business after dynamiting an old house next door: "The building blew clear across the street. It moved my building about six inches and broke some windows, but it helped save it." (13)

One of the buildings sacrificed was the Weinhard-Astoria Hotel. Astoria had been without first class accommodations until the Henry Weinhard estate purchased land on which to build an upscale hotel. The four-story structure was completed in 1910 and was situated on the southeast corner of Twelfth and Duane streets. Designed in the American Renaissance style, the hotel had eighty-one elegant guest rooms. There was even a rooftop sunroom, accessible by elevator that was enclosed by windows that could be opened during favorable weather.

The hotel was an enormous success, and at the time of the fire plans were underway for a fifth floor addition and annex. Although the hotel was of fireproof construction, it couldn't escape the hysteria sweeping the town. The Weinhard-Astoria Hotel was dynamited in the firemen's frantic efforts to stop the rapidly advancing flames. When the smoke settled, all that remained of the stylish hotel was the Ionic columned entry incised with the hotel's name. The Kiwanis and Rotary clubs later salvaged the columns and placed them in Shively Park. The park is located just over the hill off Willamsport Road, where the columns can be found in a densely wooded area, oddly out of place.

When the inferno finally died out, thirty-two city blocks had been destroyed and over two hundred shops, stores, hotels and businesses were in ruins. It was particularly distressing for business owners because many of them had been unable to pay the high price of fire insurance— less than fifty percent of the burned real estate was insured. The cost of the fire was estimated to be over $12 million.

Among the more than two hundred ruined businesses were approximately four department stores, ten women's and men's apparel shops, eleven grocery stores, twelve restaurants, five bakeries, five movie theaters, six drug stores, six furniture stores, seven meat and fish markets, six plumbing shops, twenty garage and tire stores, eleven pool halls, and four electrical shops. Along with the many other businesses that were a total loss were the Occident Hotel and both the *Morning Astorian* and the *Astoria Evening Budget*.

Three lives were reportedly lost in the fire. The president of the Bank of Commerce, Norris Staples, died of an apparent heart attack while attempting to push automobiles from the Staples Motor Company garage. Seaman Jack Cornelisen, disoriented by thick smoke, misjudged the distance to the dock at Sixteenth Street. He fell into the river and drowned. The third fatality was a suicide. An unidentified body was found the next morning hanging under one of the docks.

In the days following the fire, soldiers from nearby Fort Stevens were utilized to guard key city facilities such as bank vaults and government buildings, and to direct traffic. On the evening of December 8, as snow gently fell on the city's remains, a boat arrived from Portland with supplies and men to aid in the relief effort.

Rising from the Ashes
1922-1950

The Astoria Column, completed in 1926, stands as a sentinel over the city.

Rebuilding

The new city government worked well together in rebuilding Astoria, and a committee of ten worked long hours to devise a financing system that would forestall bankruptcy. There were no federal disaster funds in those days, but Astoria did receive large amounts of money from other Oregon communities and service organizations. Without a hint of the corruption that was present in previous administrations, the new city manager, O. A. Kratz, led the way in reconstructing an entire town. His first order of business was to replace the wooden-planked streets with pavement. In order to do this, fill would need to be brought in.

Some of this work had begun years before when residents complained that winter flood tides carried logs and debris underneath their homes and businesses. The buildings shuddered as logs banged their way between the posts and pilings. Incoming vessels brought with them a solution to this problem. The ships' ballasts were normally dumped overboard before they put on their load, so townspeople took advantage of this practice. Through the years, Astoria gradually built up the ground under the buildings with ballast from ships. "Today a good part of the town rests on rocks from Shanghai, yellow sand from Burma, volcanic ash from Alaska, and round river stones from England." (1)

Additional fill was acquired as homes were constructed on the hills above downtown. Dirt and rocks were carted down and dumped into the water, but it was a slow process. The work of filling in the town didn't begin in earnest until after the 1922 fire. Astoria's wooden streets were eventually replaced with concrete chair-walls and concrete streets, leaving extensive underground chambers conveniently used for utilities.

The fire destroyed most of the downtown streetcar tracks, so streetcars were discontinued in favor of a bus system. In June of 1924, the Astoria Transit Company began operating six Mack buses over the same route as the streetcars. The buses were able to serve areas of the city that the tracks never reached, and the fare was ten cents. (2)

The Hotel Elliott opened in 1924 on Twelfth Street, initially to accommodate post-fire construction workers. There were sixty-eight rooms and it was built in six months at a cost of approximately $75,000 ($856,000 in contemporary dollars). Large painted signs boasted "Wonderful Beds." Unfortunately, the hotel never enjoyed the status of being a grand hotel, but it remained in business until the 1960s, when it began a slow decline.

Over the years its condition went from bad to worse, until decades later when Chester Trabucco purchased the hotel and began a four million dollar restoration that was completed in 2003.

One of the most magnificent buildings to emerge following the devastating fire was the Liberty Theater. Located at the corner of Commercial and Twelfth streets, it is one of Oregon's best examples of a 1920s vaudeville/motion picture palace, with a Mediterranean exterior that continues inside with oil paintings of Venice by renowned regional artist Joseph Knowles. The theater was designed by the Portland firm of Bennes and Herzog, and opened in 1925. It offered silent movies and vaudeville acts, which included performances by luminaries such as Bing Crosby, Duke Ellington, and Ozzie Nelson. In later years, the theater provided a broad variety of theatrical presentations, films and community events. In addition to the theater, the building included street level retail space and about seven thousand square feet of office space on the second floor.

Astoria Column

The Astoria Column, completed in 1926 and rising to 125 feet, stands as a sentinel over the city. Its painted illustrations pay tribute to those people and events that forever changed the shape of the Northwest—from Captain Robert Gray's discovery of the Columbia River to the arrival of the railroad. Climbing the 164 spiral steps to the top reveals a 360-degree panorama that, on a clear day, extends 150 miles.

As early as 1898, plans were being devised to construct an observatory at the top of Coxcomb Hill. The Astoria Progressive Commercial Commission dreamed of a watchtower at the top with electric lights that would rival the Eiffel Tower of Paris. But the commission's grand plan never materialized.

In 1903, a rock quarry opened on the north side of the hill, and in 1910, the high school (now part of Clatsop Community College) was built with stone from the quarry. Thirty acres of land on Coxcomb Hill were later purchased for use as a park, and 1923 brought yet another proposed historical monument. As with earlier schemes, this one failed to get the necessary support.

In 1925, the Great Northern Railroad sponsored a cross-continental train expedition for prominent historians and financiers with the intention of dedicating historical sites along the way. Later that year, at a historical society dinner in Portland, plans for a permanent monument at Astoria were unveiled. The monument would mark the discovery of the Columbia River by Captain Robert Gray, the Lewis and Clark Expedition, and the founding of the first Euro-American settlement on the Pacific by the Astor Fur Company.

Under the direction of Ralph Budd, president of the Great Northern Railroad, Electus D. Litchfield was selected to be the architect for this monument. His drawings revealed a square base topped with a 150-foot cement column covered in a spiral of bas-relief figures twisting their way to the top. There would also be a flagpole at the top and a lighted, enclosed observation platform accessed by a circular enclosed staircase.

The monument was a gift to the city and only required Astoria to construct the platform base and pave and widen the road to the top of the hill. The rest was paid for by the Astor family and Great Northern Railroad.

Budd and Litchfield hired Italian artist Attilio Pusterla to paint a series of fourteen pictorial images on the column, from Indian villages to Oregon's statehood in 1859. He used a fresco technique called *sgraffito*, in which lines are carved in pigmented stucco. *Sgraffito* was developed during the Italian Renaissance and was used on the Trajan Column in Rome. "No known example of it exists anywhere else in the United States. And at 4,000 square feet, the Astoria Column holds one of the largest known examples of the technique in the world." (3)

The contract for construction of the column was given to A. Guthrie and Company. On April 1, 1926, the concrete foundation was poured— 300 cubic yards, twenty-five feet square, and over twelve feet deep. The column itself was poured in increments of four-foot cylindrical forms, twice a day, until completion, with all materials hauled to the top of the hill by horse and wagon.

Although a July celebration was scheduled for the completed monument, Pusterla did not finish the artwork until late October. But the gala event went on as planned, and the result was a three-day county-wide festival, complete with a Miss Columbia beauty pageant and a parade. On July 20, over 150 travelers arrived by train from Chicago, hosted by Ralph Budd. An estimated 8,000 people attended the column's dedication, which was presided over by Oregon Governor Walter Pierce.

Another kind of celebration took place on Memorial Day the following year. On May 28, 1927, Elna Christansen and George L. Baker became the first couple to exchange wedding vows at the top of the Astoria Column.

The entire wedding party, including the minister, was decked out in hiking clothes, as the bride and groom planned a honeymoon hiking trip to Crater Lake. The wedding party and most of the couple's immediate family members climbed the 164 steps to the top of the column—except the bride's father who stayed below.

For some time after the column was finished, there were concerns that stormy weather was discoloring the artwork. In fact, just a month after Pusterla completed his work on the column, Astoria experienced eighty-mile-an-hour gales and rainstorms. By March 1929 there was no doubt that weather was affecting the column's carvings. As the country plunged into the Great Depression, money to finance the repairs was a definite problem. But in 1935, the Astor family contributed $3,000, the Great Northern Railroad donated $500, and the City of Astoria added another $2,000. In July 1936, Attilio Pusterla, then seventy-four years old, arrived in Astoria to restore his beautiful artwork. (See Chapter 7, *A New Awakening*)

Swimming the Columbia

During most months of the year hypothermia is a real concern when someone accidentally tumbles into the Columbia River, so it is hard to believe that for a time the Astoria Regatta sponsored a trans-Columbia River swim. What the river temperatures were in the 1930s is a mystery, but today the average temperature of the Columbia River at Astoria ranges from forty-two degrees in January to sixty-eight degrees in August. In 1934, the first year of the event, the swim was held as a demonstration only. Wally Hug and Jim Reed, both Seaside lifeguards, were selected for their swimming abilities. They swam from Megler, Washington, to Astoria, a distance of about four and one-half miles, and are thought to be the first men to successfully do so.

The following year, in 1935, the regatta committee turned the swim into a bona fide sporting event, offering trophies and prizes for the winners. Six swimmers entered the race, one of them being Jim Reed, who won the race in two hours and thirty-five minutes. The second place finisher was Fred Rossiter of Hill Military Academy in Portland. His official time was three hours and seven minutes.

The only woman to enter the race was sixteen-year-old Laura Couch of Chinook, Washington, who finished the swim in three hours and fifty-five minutes. In 1984, Laura recalled how she felt that day:

Women's diving competition during the regatta, circa 1916. Courtesy of the Clatsop County Historical Society, Astoria, Oregon, Photo #11,445-100.

I was so proud when I was invited to ride on one of the floats. . . It was such a great experience to be a guest of honor at that beautiful event. I received a large loving cup for being 'First Woman to Swim the Columbia River at Astoria, Oregon,' and a very handsome third place trophy. (4)

The trans-Columbia swim continued to be a regatta event for several years, and then changed course with swimmers jumping into the Columbia River at Tongue Point. River swimming races were eventually discontinued altogether.

The Astoria Regatta began about 1894, but was not celebrated every year. During both World Wars, for example, the festivities did not take place. Beginning as a spirited competition among sailboats to observe the end of the fishing season, the regatta has evolved over the years into an expansive array of events. Boat races are still an important part of the festivities, but many more activities have been added to delight every member of the family—from cardboard boat races and a downtown parade, to tours of historical homes and a beer garden and street dance. The finishing touch on the final night is a magnificent fireworks display.

The Astoria Regatta began in the 1890s to celebrate the end of the fishing season. Photograph, circa 1949. Courtesy of the Clatsop County Historical Society, Astoria, Oregon, Photo #6692-101.

The Great Depression

Along with the rest of the nation, the October 1929 stock market crash plunged Oregon into the longest and most severe economic depression in history, that lasted from 1929 until the beginning of World War II.

Oregon's lumber industry, in particular, fell on difficult times when prices and demand in California continued to decline, and by 1932, eighty percent of the mills were closed in the Pacific Northwest. (5) Economic collapse kept fishing boats in the harbors, and the struggling industry never recovered. Railroads and bus lines slashed ticket prices, but hardly anyone could afford to purchase at any price, so tourism slackened and consequently hotels, restaurants, and gas stations suffered. To make matters worse, migrants from the northern plains and the south added to the number of unemployed in Oregon.

In Clatsop County, three of the five banks failed and depositors waited months and sometimes years to receive a fraction of their deposits back. The City of Astoria and the Port of Astoria defaulted on bond payments. Any tax money they were able to collect was portioned among shareholders, so there was scant left over for public service or needed improvements. With money scarce, *The Astoria Budget* newspaper for a time printed its own "money," which could be redeemed by merchants who owed the newspaper for advertising.

Ten years earlier, Astoria was a thriving community of over 14,000 people. In addition to the depression, many businesses never recovered from the 1922 fire. By 1930, Astoria's population had dropped to just over 10,000.

To assist a nation primarily of renters, Congress in 1934 created the Federal Housing Administration (FHA). Oregon's first residential loan insured under the FHA was to Mr. & Mrs. Charles Humphreys, who lived at 1267 Jerome Avenue in Astoria. The loan amount was $1,700.

Another federal program created during the Depression was the Works Progress Administration (WPA). Established in 1935, it offered work to the unemployed for various projects around the country. In 1936 Astoria benefited from the WPA when a municipal airport and a seaplane ramp were constructed on the south side of Young's Bay. The U. S. Navy used the airport during World War II, and returned it to the Port of Astoria in 1946.

Struggling canneries found a source of hope in 1937 when large schools of albacore were discovered off the coast of Oregon. Tuna production was so successful that the Columbia River Packers Association constructed two major additions to the Samuel Elmore Cannery to handle the new product. Canned with the Bumble Bee label, during the 1930s and '40s tuna surpassed salmon as the company's principal product. But tuna harvests began to diminish after 1944, and by 1950 albacore had all but disappeared from the Pacific Northwest. In the late 1940s, frozen tuna was imported from Japan and processed and canned in Astoria. Bumble Bee suspended tuna canning in 1980.

One of the most valuable of the federal programs created to help pull the country out of the Depression was the Civilian Conservation Corps (CCC). Initiated by President Roosevelt in his first month of office, the Corps trained almost three million unemployed men between the ages of seventeen and twenty-eight in jobs that affected the rural landscape of America. They were paid a dollar a day to work in such projects as reforestation, fire prevention, road and dam construction, and river stabilization. The CCC helped reclaim a large part of Clatsop Plains from encroaching sand dunes that built up as a result of the jetty constructed at the mouth of the Columbia River. The CCC built a picket fence along the beach and planted European beach grass on the dune that formed over the fence. The work re-established the coastal area as a popular recreational site.

Second World War

In an attempt to bring Astoria out of the Depression, Merle Chessman, editor of the *Astoria-Budget*, teamed in 1933 with Congressman James Mott to revive the idea of a naval base at Tongue Point. Tongue Point was established in 1921 as a submarine and destroyer base, but was never developed and sat idle for fifteen years. On August 31, 1939, the very day the Nazis invaded Poland, the base at Tongue Point was formally dedicated. Between 1939 and 1945, the site was developed into a seaplane air station. Inter-tidal land was filled in, hangars were built, a complex fuel storage system was installed, and an ordnance storage facility developed. The facility's most significant role during World War II was as a commissioning site for escort aircraft carriers (better known as "jeep flattops") that were built in large shipyards in the Portland-Vancouver area. Other wartime activities included aircrew training and routine patrol flights.

Following the war, the base at Tongue Point was converted into a moorage facility for the Ready Reserve fleet. Eight new concrete piers were built out into Cathlamet Bay, and from 1946 to 1962 the navy stored as many as five hundred mothballed ships at the facility.

World War II propelled the Pacific Northwest onto the national scene when the demand for goods and services stimulated the region's economy. Northwest seaports and air bases became points of embarkation to the Pacific for troops and supplies. Shipbuilding became a principal war industry in the Northwest, employing an estimated 150,000 workers in eighty-five shipyards in Oregon and Washington. (6) With a workforce of about fifteen hundred men, most of them local, Astoria Marine was contracted to build wooden minesweepers for the U.S. Navy, and by December 1943 had launched thirty-three ships. (7)

In 1939, local children had an effect on Astoria's shipping business. Angered by the Japanese aggression in China, local Chinese American school children joined their parents in a picket line to protest a ship being loaded with scrap iron en route to Japan. The sympathetic longshoremen honored the picket line and also voted to embargo all further scrap shipments to Japan. A similar protest took place at the Port of Portland. Shortly after Japan invaded Indochina in 1940, President Roosevelt imposed an embargo on scrap iron and steel to Japan.

In 1941, a squadron of Catalina flying boats (aircraft designed to take off and land on water), arrived in Astoria to patrol the coastline. In March 1942, disaster struck when one of the boats hit a submerged log in the Columbia River during takeoff, killing eight of the nine men on board. From then on, navy blimps from a base at Tillamook, Oregon, replaced the flying boats.

Amid growing concerns over a Japanese invasion along the West Coast, the army commandeered the ferry *Tourist No. 2*, renamed it *Octopus*, and used it to lay flotation mines in the lower river. It was actually an excellent mine layer because of its shallow draft and ability to move forward and backward. Two Army Corps of Engineer boats and several gillnet fishing boats joined the *Octopus*, laying mines until March 1942. Later, the army used the ferry to provide transportation between Fort Canby and Fort Stevens. In 1966, the ferry was sent to Alaska and used as a floating cannery.

During the war years, no ship large or small was allowed over the bar between sundown and sunrise. The Coast Guard regularly patrolled

From 1946 to 1962 the U. S. Navy stored as many as five hundred mothballed ships at Tongue Point. Photograph, circa 1950. Courtesy of the Clatsop County Historical Society, Astoria, Oregon, Photo #3971-717.

the river and convoyed all vessels through the minefields. Permits were issued for boats on the river and fishermen were heedful of the mine-field area.

Another worry was that enemy mines might drift ashore, so a civil-ian mine patrol was formed under the supervision of the navy to assist naval and military authorities in their vigilant watch for mines. After learning to distinguish the many and varied types of mines known to be deployed by the enemy, volunteers, many of them women, scoured the beaches at low tide in search of the deadly mines.

In February 1942, the *Evening Astorian Budget* reported,

> *... the army today declared the western half of Washington, Oregon, and California and the southern half of Arizona a military area from which enemy aliens and American-born Japanese will be ousted progressively to rid the Pacific coast of a potential fifth column threat.*

This affected 140,000 enemy aliens and 70,000 United States citizens of Japanese ancestry. The original registration listed ninety-nine Japanese in Clatsop County, and thirty-seven in Astoria. On May 20, the deadline for evacuation, the *Evening Astorian Budget* reported that,

> . . . the remaining Japanese population of Clatsop and Columbia counties, consisting of 60 persons, left at 9 a.m. Wednesday under military convoy for the reception center in Portland. . . Thus evacuation of all Japanese and persons of Japanese ancestry from northwestern coastal communities of Oregon had been completed.

On June 21, 1942, at 11:30 p.m., a heavily-armed Imperial Japanese Navy submarine surfaced off the coast of Gearhart, and fired an estimated seventeen rounds at Fort Stevens from its five and one-half-inch deck gun. None reached their mark; most landing in swampy terrain.

Cpl. Robert Stork was stationed at Fort Stevens at the time, having been assigned to a mine planter battery. It was his 23rd birthday when the Japanese shelled the fort. In an interview conducted soon after his 100th birthday, Stork described what happened that night:

> You'll hear all kinds of stories about how many shells were fired. We knew none of them could reach us, so no one at the fort fired back. We all marched from the barracks, and huddled by one of the buildings while they searched for the key to the ammunition locker. I think we spent two hours waiting until we even had a bullet for a gun. After that, we were required to pack 60 rounds of ammunition, a bandoleer, that we wore all the time.

Clatsop County prepared for war. Soldiers maintained jeep patrols along the beaches, and armed Coast Guard men also patrolled the beaches with dogs and horses. To cut down the light visible at sea, nightly "dim-out" practices were in effect along the entire Pacific coast from Canada to Mexico, as far inland in some places as 150 miles. This made nighttime travel tricky. Robert Lovell remembered driving his car "with little slits for headlights," and being able to go "about five miles per hour at night." (8) And everyone confronted rationing—meat, oils, sugar, canned goods, shoes, and gasoline.

Tire rationing went into effect in 1942, wielding a blow to the logging industry. Trucks that normally required 250 tires a month were allotted thirty-eight tires the first month, and not a single pound of rubber would be allowed "for tires for America's 30,000,000 automobiles." (9)

The country began a scrap rubber drive, calling on civilians to bring in all the scrap rubber they could find. Clatsop County residents heeded the call, and by July 1942 they had amassed a total of 688,480 pounds of rubber, well above the state average. To conserve rubber, civilians were requested not to exceed a speed of forty miles per hour. Tire rationing was suspended in January 1945.

With most of the young men off to war, the country entertained the idea of employing women. A trial survey was conducted in Clatsop County in February 1942, the first in the nation. Four hundred interviewers from the federal employment agency went house to house in Astoria asking women to fill out forms indicating their vocational experience, skills, and abilities. By May of 1942 there were more women wanting to work than there were jobs. Seventy percent of Clatsop County women had registered (6,047), and seven canneries indicated they would employ about twelve hundred women during the fishing season. With so many women now in the workforce, the community council recommended applying for funds to finance a day nursery.

It wasn't only women who were finding employment. With tuna and salmon turning up in record numbers, many high school and grade school children worked in the canneries. Even after school started in the fall of 1942, students were permitted to continue working for about the first ten days of school, "until the majority of Astoria's great salmon pack has been saved for food for the armed forces." (10) The *Evening Astorian Budget* reported on September 8 that "of the 97 working in canneries now, it was disclosed that a bit more than half are girls."

The record numbers of chinook salmon were somewhat of a surprise, coming five years after the completion of the Bonneville Dam on the Columbia River. Fishermen brought in catches of up to 6,000 pounds, with one fisherman catching 5,322 pounds in a single drift.

Cable TV

Cable television was invented and developed in 1948 by Ed Parsons, an engineer and Astoria radio station operator, apparently because Parsons could not say "no" to his wife. Parsons recalled attending a broadcast convention in Chicago a few years earlier where his wife saw a television demonstration for the first time. Even though there were no television stations on the West Coast at the time, she told Parsons on the way home that she wanted a television. About a year later, it was announced that a station would be built in Seattle by KRSC.

Parsons eventually ordered a television set for his wife, a nine-inch black and white model that he bought "primarily because it was a hi-fi AM/FM and a record player." (11) Parsons paid $1,000 or more for the set and said that to afford it his wife "had to do without other things." (12)

They lived in an apartment in the Astor Hotel (on Fourteenth Street between Commercial and Duane) where Parsons discovered he could get a television signal from the roof. On Thanksgiving Day in 1948, he mounted an antenna to the hotel's rooftop, stringing lines down to his living room television. While Parsons adjusted the aerial on the roof, his wife used a walkie-talkie to report the reception in the living room. "Reception was not of a quality that would be salable today, but we received a picture and started attracting guests," said Parsons. (13) Using coaxial cable, he wired the signal across the street to the roof of Poole's Music Store (on the southwest corner of Duane and Four- teenth), making Poole's the first documented cable customer in the United States.

Parsons eventually sent the signal to a few friends and ultimately erected an antenna on Coxcomb Hill, feeding the picture down the south slope. By May 1950, approximately seventy-five homes in Astoria were connected to the cable. (14)

Unfortunately, Parsons wasn't as adept in the financial realm as he was in electronics, and by 1953 he was bankrupt. A group of Astorians bought the cable system, eventually constructing a large, multi-channel cable and upgrading the equipment. Within several years, almost every home in Astoria was receiving cable television.

Astoria in 1962 received a plaque from the National Community Television Association commemorating cable television's beginnings in Astoria. In May 1968, a brass marker was unveiled on Coxcomb Hill, and a plaque was presented to Ed Parsons, recognizing him as the founder of cable television. By 1970, five million homes across the con- tinent were connected to cable television. (15)

Modern Times
1950-present day

The Astoria Bridge spans four and one-tenth miles across the Columbia River.

Falling Asleep

Astoria's population increased during the war years, and in 1950 over 12,000 people called Astoria home. But the war-era jobs eventually came to an end, and by the 1950s most of the canneries in Astoria were but a distant memory—unable to compete with Alaska, the last Oregon salmon cannery closed in 1979. People left town in search of employment, and commercial vacancy rates downtown rose to as high as forty percent. Astoria began a steady decline, and then simply went to sleep. The 1983 population was 9,775.

A short boost in the local economy occurred during the Korean War (1950-53) when the Astoria Marine Construction Company became the country's first producer of 165-foot AMS minesweepers. These boats, made entirely of wood, were constructed with non-magnetic materials to avoid detection and destruction by enemy mines. Astoria Marine hired over four hundred men to build these new minesweepers without using a single piece of magnetic material—a task that required many of the parts to be specially made.

Astoria Marine also assisted in the business of de-mothballing the ships at Tongue Point that had been sitting idle since the Second World War. Once restored, the ships were given to South Korea, Taiwan and other allies of the United States. The navy base closed in 1959, and by 1960, Astoria Marine's workforce was down to only fifteen. (1)

By 1962, Tongue Point Naval Air Station was transferred to the General Services Administration as excess property. Since then, the property has had several different owners, including agencies of the federal government, the Oregon Division of State Lands, and private parties. In 1964, the Tongue Point Job Corps Center opened. The center is the only one in the country to offer a seamanship vocational trade in the specialty area of maritime transportation, which is certified by the U. S. Coast Guard.

Where Are They Now?

What has become of the Chinookan people who for centuries inhabited the western most region of the Columbia?

After the encroachment of their land by disease-carrying European Americans, and the subsequent demise of thousands of their people, few Clatsops or Chinooks were left to carry on the native traditions of their people. About two hundred members of the Clatsop tribe in Oregon aligned themselves with the Nehalems, forming the Clatsop-Nehalem Confederated Tribe.

In an attempt to assimilate native American Indians into mainstream America, the U.S. government in the 1950s passed legislation that ended trusteeship of 109 tribes or bands across the country. Sixty-two of them were native to Oregon. The process was called "termination," and instead of emancipation for tribal members, the result was cultural, political and economic devastation.

In a move to reestablish a trust relationship, the Legislative Commission on Indian Services was created in Oregon in 1975. The commission holds meetings to learn what problems the Indians are facing and to discuss possible solutions. Beginning in 1977, restoration of some Oregon tribes began to take place, and today there are nine federally-recognized tribes in the state of Oregon. A representative from each tribe is invited to sit on the commission. The Clatsops, however, are not a recognized tribe, and so are not represented.

Conditions for granting recognition to a tribe are complex and require a lengthy documentation process. However, once a tribe receives federal recognition, its members benefit by becoming eligible for health care, fishing rights, access to federal grants, and sometimes, land.

In 1934, as a result of the Indian Reorganization Act (enacted to help preserve native cultures), the Chinook tribe was granted land and received fishing rights. However, they didn't occupy the land because it was on the Quinault Indian Reservation, far from their home lands on the Columbia River. In 1967, the Bureau of Indian Affairs delisted about 100 tribes, including the Chinook, alleging it didn't have a reservation and, therefore, was not an official tribe.

The Chinooks unsuccessfully appealed the decision. In 1978, a Branch of Acknowledgment and Research was created and so began a twenty-three-year process by the Chinooks to regain recognition. Finally, on January 3, 2001, the federal government formally recognized the Chinook Nation. But it didn't end there. When the Quinault Tribe filed an appeal, alleging the Chinooks had not followed correct procedures, Secretary of the Interior Gale Norton subjected the appeal to a full review. Apparently the Chinooks hold more than half of the Quinault reservation allotments, so federal recognition of the Chinook Nation was seen as a threat to Quinault control of the reservation's resources, which include a lucrative casino. When the appeals process was completed, the tribe received word that its recognition had been denied.

Both the Clatsops and Chinooks continue their decades-long pursuit for federal recognition.

Modern Coast Guard

Coast Guard Group/Air Station Astoria was established in August 1964 at Tongue Point Naval Air Station. In 1966, they moved to their current location at the Warrenton/Astoria Airport where they oversee all operational units from Grays Harbor, Washington, to Garibaldi, Oregon.

Station Cape Disappointment is located in Washington at the mouth of the Columbia River, where strong outgoing tides collide with large incoming swells, creating perilous surf conditions with waves often exceeding twenty to thirty feet. With fifty crew members assigned, Station Cape Disappointment is the largest Coast Guard search and rescue station on the Northwest Coast, providing assistance to commercial and recreational mariners within fifty nautical miles of the Columbia River entrance. With two forty-seven-foot search and rescue life boats, they respond to three- to-four hundred calls for assistance every year. (2) They also provide maritime law enforcement near the approaches to the Columbia River.

The first life saving station at Cape Disappointment was built on the site of Fort Canby in 1877 and for five years was manned entirely by volunteers. The Life Saving Service took over in 1882, and in 1915, it merged with the Revenue Marine Cutter Service to form the United States Coast Guard.

The existing station was first occupied in February 1967, and since 1980, has also been the site of the National Motor Life Boat School, the only school in the country for rough weather surf rescue operations. Twice a year, the school offers a four-week class for twelve people who are striving for heavy weather or surfman certification. In addition to the U. S. Coast Guard, students from the Canadian Coast Guard and other countries attend the school.

Congress in 1984 mandated that the Coast Guard establish a helicopter rescue swimmer program for the purpose of training selected Coast Guard personnel in rescue swimming skills. By 1987, rescue swimmers had been assigned to six air stations around the country, including Astoria. In 1995, when it was becoming increasingly apparent that rescue swimmers were needed to offer assistance in extremely hazardous conditions—high surf and seas, caves, rescuing victims trapped on slippery rocks or steep cliffs, it was recommended that additional, advanced training be provided in techniques and equipment that rescue swimmers do not normally receive. Astoria was selected as the best location for this training, offering a rugged coastline, demanding surf, and prevailing high seas. The tasks required of these swimmers are extremely difficult. Forty to fifty percent of those who enter the swimming program do not complete the course.

Twice a year pilots, hoist operators, flight mechanics and rescue swimmers from all Coast Guard stations receive advanced rescue swimmer training in Astoria. Most of this training is performed from the "Jay Hawk" HH-60 helicopters in sea conditions twenty- to twenty-five feet high. The Coast Guard also utilizes the facilities at the Astoria Aquatic Center, where they hone their swimming skills and practice underwater techniques.

Astoria is the home port for the Coast Guard cutters *Alert, Steadfast* and *Elm*. When not in port, the 210-foot *Alert* and *Steadfast*, each with about seventy-five crewmembers, patrol the waters of the Pacific Ocean

Forty-seven-foot U. S. C. G. motor life boat. Station Cape Disappointment is the largest Coast Guard search and rescue station on the Northwest Coast. Courtesy Larry Kellis Photography.

from Mexico to Canada, enforcing federal fisheries and vessel safety laws. They also enforce laws regarding illegal immigration and contraband, and are prepared to respond to search and rescue incidents at sea. In addition, they have been called upon to undertake the latest Coast Guard mission of homeland security. The *Elm* is a 225-foot seagoing buoy tender, with the primary mission of servicing and maintaining aids to navigation along the coasts of Oregon and Washington. One month per year the *Elm* engages in fisheries law enforcement, and can be deployed for environmental clean-up in the event of a major oil spill.

Navigating the River

Today's Columbia River bar pilots are at the ready to guide enormous ships through one of the most hazardous stretches of water in the world, where it is not unusual to find twenty-five to thirty-foot seas and sixty to seventy knot winds. They maintain two pilot boats and one helicopter on standby at all times. Because the seas are unpredictable, it can take from two to six hours to make the transit into or out of the river. Federal law requires all vessels entering the river to carry a licensed pilot while crossing this seventeen-mile stretch of water. The master of an American ship, if licensed by the Coast Guard, may do his or her own pilotage.

Vessels on the Columbia can call for a pilot at Astoria.

River Pilot: 1 long and 3 short whistles

Bar Pilot: 1 long, 2 short, and 1 long whistle

Launch: 1 long and 2 short whistles

In 1996, bar pilots started experimenting with helicopter boarding, and in 1999, began using a helicopter full time to board incoming vessels, weather permitting. Helicopters are able to land on about forty percent of the ships. If a ship's deck cannot accommodate a helicopter landing, the pilot is lowered by hoist. Helicopter boardings typically take place five to ten miles out to sea, giving the pilot ample time to evaluate a ship's condition and capability before it crosses the bar. This is the only place in the United States where a helicopter boarding is routinely used. Its use has allowed the pilots to keep the bar open in more extreme weather.

Above*: Pilot Boat heading out.* Below*: Pilot boat alongside vessel. Pilots clamber aboard moving vessels via a dangling ladder.*

The bar pilot takes control of the ship and guides it in as far as Astoria. If the ship is continuing to an upriver port, the bar pilot is relieved on the bridge by a river pilot who will make the passage to one of the upriver ports. The river pilot is responsible for navigating vessels along the winding river from Astoria to upriver ports. Pilots also determine a safe draft to maximize use of the forty-three-foot deep and six hundred-foot wide channel—sometimes the distance between the hull of a ship and the bottom of the river is a mere two feet. When a vessel is heading out to sea, the river pilot transfers the vessel to a bar pilot in Astoria. It is exciting to watch these skillful guides leap from a small pilot boat, grab a dangling ladder, and then clamber aboard a massive moving freighter.

Today's bar pilots have from ten to fifteen years experience at sea and must have had at least two years experience as a ship's master to qualify as a bar pilot. This is the highest licensing standard for admission into pilotage in the United States. Captain George Flavel, who was granted a pilot's license in 1851, initiated this high standard by requiring all of his subordinates to have been ship's masters. River pilots must first serve as tugboat captains on the Columbia for two years and become skilled at the 104 course changes between Portland and the Pacific Ocean.

Bridge to Nowhere

For decades, discussions took place about the possibility of constructing a bridge across the Columbia River. Finally, in 1953, a partnership formed with the Port of Astoria, Oregon Highway Department, Washington State Toll Bridge Authority, and Pacific County, Washington, with a mission to learn how to build such a bridge. In 1957, the Oregon and Washington legislatures together funded $100,000 to prepare the plans for the bridge, and four years later, both legislatures agreed to fully fund the project.

Oregon Governor Mark Hatfield, in a ceremony in August 1962, dug the first shovel full of dirt to initiate construction of the bridge, and in July 1966, more than 30,000 people watched as Governor Hatfield and Washington Governor Dan Evans cut the ceremonial ribbon to mark the opening of the new bridge.

The Astoria Bridge (commonly referred to as the Astoria-Megler Bridge) spans a distance of four and one-tenth miles across the Columbia River, and when completed was the longest continuous truss bridge in the world with a main arch 1,232 feet long. The bridge can withstand

When the Astoria Bridge was first constructed, some doubted it would ever pay for itself. By 1993, tolls had paid off the bonds and more than 1.6 million vehicles crossed the "bridge to nowhere."

wind gusts of 150 miles per hour, and the concrete piers are built to handle the constant flow of the river rushing by at nine miles per hour.

A toll was initiated to pay off the debt for the bridge, although many skeptics, wondering who would want to take a bridge from a small town to a vacant shore, predicted it would never pay for itself. However, on December 24, 1993, the bonds were paid off and the tollbooths removed. That same year, more than 1.6 million vehicles crossed the "bridge to nowhere."

Hurray for Hollywood

Astoria's unique character and surroundings have been the home of many Hollywood productions. Among the movies filmed in Astoria are *The Goonies, Short Circuit, Benji the Hunted, Come See the Paradise, Kindergarten Cop, Teenage Mutant Ninja Turtles III, Free Willy, The Ring II,* and *Into the Wild.*

Stephen Spielberg's *The Goonies,* filmed in 1984, has achieved cult

*The Liberty Theater, built in 1925, was transformed
into a 667-seat performing arts center.*

status and draws visitors to Astoria just to see its locations, especially the Goonies' house, and the historic county jail behind the courthouse. *Short Circuit* was filmed a year later and showed several robots jumping off the Astoria Bridge. Ally Sheedy's character lived in the house at 197 Hume Street. Astor School at Thirty-fifth and Franklin was the main location for *Kindergarten Cop* in 1990. The movie company hired local artists to paint murals on the outside walls of the school. These colorful murals have been maintained over the years and still look as though they were freshly painted. The Fourteenth Street dock was turned into a fish market in 1992 for the movie *Free Willy*, and Jason James Richter's character lived in the house at the corner of Thirty-fourth and Harrison. Filmed in 2004, *The Ring II* featured many local Astorians and business owners. Naomi Watts' character lived in a house at the corner of Tenth and Jerome.

A tour book of movie locations is available from the Clatsop County Historical Society or from the Astoria-Warrenton Area Chamber of Commerce.

The Goonies *has achieved cult status and draws many visitors to Astoria, particularly to see this house on Thirty-eighth Street and the historic county jail, below.*

A Bright Red Trolley

In 1996, when Burlington Northern Santa Fe Railway announced it was pulling out of Astoria, the move paved the way for Astoria to gain ownership of the rails, which resulted in the creation of the river walk, and the arrival of the Riverfront Trolley two years later.

Built in St. Louis in 1914, *Old Number 300* clanged its way up and down the streets of San Antonio, Texas, for nearly twenty years. When the city transportation system converted to automobiles, the town's electric trolleys were gradually retired, and *Old Number 300* was given to the San Antonio Museum Association.

In 1998, representatives from Astoria discovered the trolley in disrepair, with a rotting roof and an entire wall that was nearly gone. But the electric motor hummed, so the delegation was hopeful that the trolley could be salvaged. San Antonio agreed to lease the trolley to the City of Astoria for a dollar a year. An estimated three hundred volunteers worked more than 3,000 hours over a five-month period rebuilding and restoring the forty-passenger car.

A generator at one end powers the trolley back and forth along a three mile track from the Port of Astoria to Pier 39. When the trolley reaches the end of the line, everyone on board stands up and flips their hinged seat backs so they can face the other way for the return trip.

A brass bell clangs at every intersection as the red and green trolley rolls along Astoria's scenic riverfront. Operated solely by volunteers, friendly conductors provide commentary of local history along the route. It costs a dollar a ride and passengers can remain on board as long as they wish. The trolley carried more than 250,000 people during its first six years of operation.

In 2005, the San Antonio Museum of Art board of directors voted to approve the sale of *Old Number 300* to the City of Astoria. The price was $50,000, paid almost entirely with donations, and with the City of Astoria contributing $5,000.

A New Awakening

Although no canneries remain in Astoria, remnants of the piers that once anchored them can be seen for miles along the waterfront. The only cannery building still standing is at Pier 39. The Hanthorn Cannery, originally built in 1875, has been renovated to accommodate a number of businesses.

Riverfront Trolley. Traveling along Astoria's scenic riverfront and operated solely by volunteers, Old Number 300 *carried more than a quarter million people during its first six years of operation.*

Fishing remains a vital part of the local economy, and Astoria is one of the top seafood ports in the country—plants process fish, shrimp, oysters, and Dungeness crab. One of the larger facilities is Bornstein's, which operates plants from Alaska to Southern Oregon.

The Duncan Law Seafood Consumer Center is located at Twentieth and Marine Drive, next to the Oregon State University (OSU) seafood laboratory. For nearly forty years, former OSU professor Duncan Law worked to procure the funds needed to create a place for research and development for the benefit of consumers and the fishing industry. The center opened in 1998 and is equipped with a demonstration kitchen where consumers can learn how to buy and prepare the salmon, albacore, sturgeon, crab and shrimp that arrive fresh to Astoria's docks. There is also a large conference room available for community functions and private parties.

As the twenty-first century dawned, it provided a new awakening for the slumbering city—the Lewis and Clark Bicentennial. Outsiders began to suddenly take notice of the small community at the mouth of the Columbia River, and as they did, so did developers and those with an eye toward the future. Downtown Astoria took on a fresh new look as eclectic shops, galleries, and restaurants moved into previously abandoned storefronts. Locals reminisced about the past and began taking an interest in Astoria's lengthy history. As a result, restoration projects began to occur all over town.

The Astoria Column, a prominent marker on the city's landscape and popular tourist attraction, had been neglected for years. Although listed in 1974 on the National Register of Historic Places, the column was closed two years later for structural repairs after an x-ray revealed numerous cracks. The mural, untended for thirty years, was also in dire need of restoration.

For another twenty years the artwork continued to deteriorate while experts consulted one another about the best way to proceed. By 1995, when Friends of the Astoria Column, headed by president Jordan Schnitzer, stepped in with plans to restore the column, the pictures were barely discernible. Renovations began the same year and were completed in 2004. The end result is beautifully restored artwork, a seismically-stabilized column, a new plaza with pavers, paths with seating, and spotlights that illuminate the column by night. A rededication ceremony on July 10, 2004—almost seventy-eight years to the day after its initial dedication in 1926—was presided over by Oregon's First Lady Mary Oberst, Astoria Mayor Willis Van Dusen, and Jordan Schnitzer. The final touch took place in 2009 with the replacement of the spiral staircase.

In the first year after the column was built, Astoria's Chamber of Commerce reported hundreds of tourists requesting information each week about the column. Today, "an estimated 350,000 people a year visit the column, placing it among Oregon's top 10 tourist sites." (3)

Another major project was the Liberty Theater renovation. Located at the corner of Commercial and Twelfth streets, the theater first opened in 1925 to silent movies and vaudeville acts. It sat neglected for many years until Liberty Restoration, Inc., a private non-profit organization, purchased the building in 2000 and launched a multi-million dollar restoration. The theater has been transformed into a 677-seat performing arts center. In 2003, the theater was featured on Home and Garden Television's "Restore America: A Salute to Preservation."

Originally built in 1924 to house post-fire construction workers, the Hotel Elliott has been renovated and boasts a rooftop garden with 360-degree views. The hotel was placed on the National Trust for Historic Preservation's list of two hundred historic hotels.

Another impressive restoration effort was the Hotel Elliott across the street from the Liberty Theater. Built in 1924 to house post-fire construction workers, the building went through decades of disrepair until Chester Trabucco purchased the building and began a $4 million renovation that was completed in 2003. The deteriorating structure was turned into a thirty-two-room upscale boutique hotel with luxurious, comfortable furnishings, and top-of-the-line mattresses that live up to the repainted "Wonderful Beds" sign on the outside wall. There is also a rooftop garden with 360-degree views. The original registration desk is in the lobby, along with a 1920s photograph of the original owners. The hotel was placed on the National Trust for Historic Preservation's list of two hundred historic hotels.

Not to be left behind, the Columbia River Maritime Museum, founded in 1962, underwent a six million dollar expansion that included the addition of an exhibit of a full-size, forty-four-foot Coast Guard motor lifeboat churning through a simulated wave. Outside the museum, the retired lightship *Columbia* is open for tours. The museum was the first nationally accredited maritime museum in the western United States, and its seven galleries house one of the most extensive nautical collections on the West Coast. Visitors to the museum also have the opportunity to walk the bridge of a World War II warship.

In 2005, hundreds pitched in to help build a remarkable new playground in Tapiola Park. In just six days volunteers erected a distinctive playground that evokes the area's history. Designed with input from local school children, the park's play structures replicate Fort Clatsop, the Astoria Bridge, the Flavel House Museum, and other nearby landmarks. Through local fundraising activities, the citizens of Astoria raised about $150,000 for the project, the city contributed $7,000, and the Tapiola Playground committee raised $205,000. In September 2005, the Tapiola Playground project received the 2005 Oregon Recreation and Park Association Design Award, and in November, the League of Oregon Cities bestowed its annual Award for Excellence on this extraordinary project. Tapiola Park is located on West Marine Drive.

Commerce along the Columbia River began centuries ago with the Chinookan people. That tradition of trade continues today, but massive oceangoing vessels have replaced the Indian canoes. Much of the region's economy depends on this maritime trade, and the Columbia River is the United States' largest wheat export system, handling forty

Tapiola Park, on West Marine Drive, includes replicas of Fort Clatsop, the Astoria Bridge, and other nearby landmarks. The League of Oregon Cities bestowed its annual Award For Excellence on this extraordinary project.

per cent of all U.S. wheat exports. In addition, various types of vessels transport an average of $14 billion worth of cargo each year—tugboats towing barges, bulk carriers heavily laden with grain, container ships with boxcars heaped high, car carriers loaded with thousands of cars—a never-ending parade of ships bypassing Astoria for upriver ports like Longview and Portland.

In recent years, major cruise lines joined the procession of cargo carriers, making Astoria a regular stop to and from the northern waters of the Pacific. In 2004, a total of eight large cruise ships visited Astoria. On a single day in September, three ships docked or laid anchor, bringing 7,000 passengers and crewmembers to the streets of Astoria. The next year arrived with fourteen ships, bringing perhaps as many as 25,000 people to town.

More than two hundred years have passed since Captain Robert Gray sailed his ship across the Columbia River bar and into the history books. Gray, more concerned with trade than with exploration, wrote in his log: "So ends." And Ulysses S. Grant, equally unimpressed with the area in 1850, concluded in a letter to his wife: "So much for Astoria." They would both be shocked if they visited Astoria today.

Astoria's vast history, its ties to the Lewis & Clark Expedition, and its colorfully-restored Victorian homes dotting the hillside, have all led to a flood of tourists discovering Astoria. May 2003 brought to Astoria the Lewis & Clark Explorer train. Funded through grants and private donations to transport visitors to Astoria during the peak Lewis & Clark bicentennial years, it chugged along Burlington Northern's abandoned rails, hugging the Columbia River from Portland to Astoria, ending its journey in front of the boarded-up brick train depot abandoned decades ago.

This 1924 train depot, given to the Columbia River Maritime Museum in 1987, was historically restored in 2013, and is now the Barbey Maritime Center for Research and Industry. Named for a local family with a long history in the salmon packing industry, it promotes maritime skills and the culture of Columbia River life.

Restaurants and shops have taken the place of riverfront canneries, and the once-polluted site of the former Clatsop Mill was reclaimed and developed into a quaint riverfront neighborhood. On Sundays between May and October, Twelfth Street is closed to traffic and the "Sunday Market" materializes. Vendors display fresh produce and handcrafted wares, musicians offer free entertainment, and there are enough food booths to satisfy everyone's palate. All products sold must be grown, picked or made by the vendors. Astoria's outdoor market is the second largest in the state of Oregon. Only Portland's is bigger. During the twenty-two week market in 2005, vendors collectively realized one and one-half million dollars in sales.

Astoria today is a city of about ten thousand. It may not have reached the "seaport of the Northwest" status that it so strongly desired, but it might be better off. Curious tourists can come and go, giving a boost to the local economy, but Astoria will hopefully remain what it has been for more than a century—a working man's town, where residents have a comforting sense of community and of knowing their neighbors, where family-run businesses are the norm, and where fishing boats keep pace with the tides.

CLATSOP MILL COMPANY 1890.

NOTICE THE EARLY STREET CAR DRAWN BY A HORSE.

Clatsop Mill Company, circa 1890. The site is now an upscale riverfront neighborhood. Courtesy of the Clatsop County Historical Society, Astoria, Oregon, Photo #253-625.

Astoria Area
Self-Guided Tour

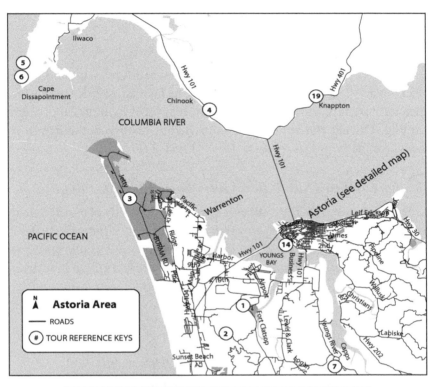

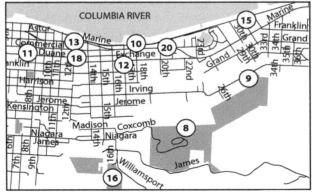

Detail of Astoria.

Astoria area self-guided tour maps.
Circled numbers correspond to tour highlights
described on the following pages.

If you are lucky enough to find yourself in Astoria for more than a few hours, take advantage of the numerous scenic and historic attractions in the area. To get you started, listed here is a selection of twenty things to see and do in and near Astoria.

(1) *Fort Clatsop* (southwest of Astoria, off US 101)

This is where the Lewis and Clark Expedition wintered from December 7, 1805 until March 23, 1806. The facility includes the reconstructed fort, a visitor center/museum, historical exhibits, and canoe landing. During the summer months, living history demonstrations depict fort activities. Admission fee. 503-861-2471.

(2) *Fort To Sea Trail* (between Fort Clatsop and Sunset Beach)

This trail wends its way through the woods south of Fort Clatsop to Sunset Beach, traveling through much of the same forest, fields and dunes that the Corps traveled. While the trail is navigable in any weather, rain can make the trail slick in places and muddy in others. Also note that the trail traverses up and down steep ravines. Approximately 6.5 miles one way. Shuttles are sometimes available, otherwise a cab or wait car should be arranged.

(3) *Fort Stevens State Park* (Ridge Road, Hammond)

The original fort was constructed during the Civil War. Visitors can learn its history at the museum and explore abandoned gun batteries. This 3,700 acre state park has picnic facilities, nature trails, miles of beaches, lakes, boating, camping, swimming, and more than nine miles of paved bicycle paths. Campground is open year-around with over 600 campsites for campers, recreational vehicles and tents. Day use and camping fees. 800-551-6949.

(4) *Fort Columbia State Park* (in Washington, two miles west of Astoria bridge)

Fort Columbia State Park is a 593-acre day-use historical park with sixty-four hundred feet of freshwater shoreline on the Columbia River. The park celebrates a military site that constituted the harbor defense of the Columbia River from 1896 to 1947. The fort was fully manned and operational through three wars. The park includes an interpretive

Examples of Victorian-style architecture are plentiful throughout Astoria. This house is on Franklin Avenue in Uppertown.

center focusing on fort history and Chinook culture, a self-guided trail, and the Commander's House Museum, which is filled with era-appropriate furnishings. Camping is not allowed, but two historical homes are available as vacation rentals. 888-226-7688. Summer and winter hours.

⑤ *Cape Disappointment State Park* (*two miles southwest of Ilwaco, WA*)

Cape Disappointment is a 2,023-acre camping park on the Long Beach Peninsula, fronted by the Pacific Ocean and looking into the mouth of the Columbia River. The park offers yurts, cabins, historic vacation homes, twenty-seven miles of ocean beach, two lighthouses, an interpretive center, and hiking trails. Summer and winter hours. Campsite information: 888-226-7688.

House on Twelfth Street.

⑥ *Lewis And Clark Interpretive Center* (Cape Disappointment State Park)

This interpretive center sits high on the cliffs of the park. A series of mural-sized "timeline" panels guide visitors through the westward journey of the Lewis and Clark Expedition using sketches, paintings, photographs and the words of Corps members themselves. Additional displays focus on local maritime and military history. Admission fee. 360-642-3078.

⑦ *Young's River Falls* (eight miles south of Astoria)

Young's River was discovered in 1792 by William Robert Broughton of the Vancouver Expedition and named for Sir George Young of the Royal Navy. The first ground pulp mill in Oregon was at Young's River Falls. Directions: Highway 202 south to the town of Olney. At Olney, turn right onto Young's River Loop Road. In four miles, turn left where the falls are signed. The 65-foot falls are visible from the parking area.

House on Kensington Avenue.

(8) *Astoria Column* (*Coxcomb Hill*)

In a wooded 30-acre park and situated on Astoria's tallest hill, the Astoria Column presents a spectacular view of the city and surrounding rivers, bay, forest, mountains and Pacific Ocean. The column commemorates the westward sweep of discovery and migration. Built in 1926, it is 125 feet high with 164 steps winding to the top. Open dawn to dusk. Visiting the park or climbing the Column is free. Parking is $5 per vehicle, which is good for one year. Directions: Follow signs and white-painted columns on Fourteenth or Sixteenth streets. 503-325-2963.

(9) *Cathedral Tree/Column Trail* (*Twenty-eighth & Irving*)

From Twenty-eighth & Irving, hike this forested trail one-third mile to the Cathedral Tree, a Sitka spruce some two hundred feet tall and estimated to be over three hundred years old. Continue one mile further along the trail to the Astoria Column.

(10) *Columbia River Maritime Museum* *(Seventeenth & Marine Drive)*

This museum of national distinction has interactive exhibits for visitors of all ages. Entrance fee includes a tour of the Lightship *Columbia*, docked at the Seventeenth Street pier. Before buoys lighted the way, this small vessel sat anchored at the entrance to the river, guiding ships safely into the channel. Admission fee. 503-325-2323.

(11) *Flavel House Museum* *(Eighth & Duane)*

Built in 1885 by Captain George Flavel for his retirement, this Queen Anne style Victorian home and its period furnishings enable visitors to imagine life in Astoria at the turn of the last century. It has been operating as a museum since 1951. Captain Flavel became the first licensed Master Mariner to be granted a pilotage license for the Columbia River bar, and eventually became Astoria's first millionaire. Admission fee. 503-325-2203.

(12) *Heritage Museum* *(Sixteenth & Exchange)*

The museum features permanent exhibits interpreting Clatsop County's history. Built in 1904 on the site of the 1811 Astor company burial grounds, this neo-classic style structure was Astoria's city hall until 1939. For twenty years it was the home of the Columbia River Maritime Museum. Admission fee. 503-325-2203.

(13) *Liberty Theater* *(Twelfth & Commercial)*

Now a performing arts center, this restored theater was built in 1925. It is one of Oregon's best examples of a 1920s vaudeville/motion picture palace, with a Mediterranean exterior that continues inside with oil paintings of Venice by renowned regional artist Joseph Knowles. It originally offered silent movies and vaudeville acts. 503-325-5922.

(14) *Tapiola Park Playground* *(West Marine Drive & South Denver Street)*

Designed with input from local school children, this remarkable playground was built by volunteers in just six days. The structures replicate the area's history, including Fort Clatsop, the Astoria Bridge, and Flavel House Museum, all with a view of Young's Bay.

House on Grand Avenue.

Take your children or grandchildren to this one-of-a-kind park that received the 2005 Oregon Recreation and Park Association Design Award, and the League of Oregon Cities' annual Award for Excellence.

⑮ *Uppertown Firefighters Museum* (Thirtieth & Marine)

Contains an extensive collection of firefighting equipment dating from 1877 to 1963. On display are hand-pulled, horse drawn and motorized vehicles, fire fighting equipment, photos and memorabilia. Astoria's history of disastrous fires is told in photographs and artifacts. The building was constructed in 1896 to serve as part of the North Pacific Brewery. In 1928 the site was rebuilt by the city of Astoria for service as Uppertown Firestation #2. Admission fee. 503-325-2203.

⑯ *Shively Park* (Williamsport Road)

A woodsy urban park dating back to 1898. For Astoria's 1911 centennial celebration the city built an amphitheater, a reconstruction of Fort Astoria, and exhibition halls, although none of them remain today. You will find a community hall, trails, a small play structure, picnic shelters, and the entrance arch from the old Weinhard-Astoria Hotel, which was moved to the park after downtown Astoria burned in 1922.

⑰ *Victorian Homes* (hillsides of Astoria)

Often referred to as the "Little San Francisco of the Northwest," Astoria is renowned for its picture book Victorian homes and steep hills. A walking (or driving) tour allows visitors to see scores of beautifully preserved nineteenth and early twentieth century private homes and public buildings, many of them listed on the National Register of Historic Places. One day of touring will take you past more than seventy-four historical buildings and sites. A booklet of historic homes is available from the Astoria-Warrenton Area Chamber of Commerce. 503-325-6311.

⑱ *Astoria Sunday Market* (Twelfth Street between Marine & Exchange)

Beginning with Mother's Day and continuing to October, a three-block stretch of Twelfth Street is transformed when more than one hundred vendors offer fresh fruits and vegetables, garden goods, art, crafts, music and food for every palate. Astoria's outdoor market is the second largest in the state of Oregon. Sundays from ten to three. 503-325-1010.

*Today, Captain Flavel's home at Eighth and Duane
is a museum open to the public.*

(19) *Knappton Cove Heritage Center* (*in Washington, three miles east of the Astoria Bridge*)

Knappton Cove was once the site of the U.S. Quarantine Station, often referred to as the "Ellis Island of the Columbia." It opened in 1899, and all ships entering the river were boarded and inspected for disease. If fumigation or quarantine were warranted, ships anchored at Knappton Cove. The station closed in 1938. In 1980 the former quarantine station was accepted to the National Register of Historic Places. The property is privately owned, and the museum is open to the public at different times throughout the year. 503-738-5206.

(20) *Astoria Aquatic Center* (*Twentieth & Marine Drive*)

When you need a break from sight-seeing, the Astoria Aquatic Center might be the place to go. It has a lap pool, recreation pool, spa pool and kiddie's pool. There is a water slide and lazy river, and also a fitness room with weight machines and free weights. In addition to men's and women's locker rooms, there are family changing rooms for those with small children. Open to the public, admission fee. 503-325-7027.

Self-Guided Tour
Along the River

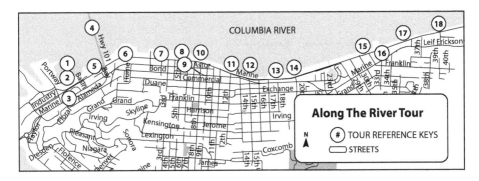

Circled numbers correspond to tour highlights described below.

Whether walking, taking the trolley, or riding a bike, Astoria's riverfront is an amazing place to visit. Not only are the views of the river and surrounding mountains spectacular, you will get a sense of the city's past, when salmon was king and the fishing and canning industries thrived.

As you make your way along the river, notice the wood pilings in the water. These are the only remaining remnants of the numerous salmon canneries that once lined the riverbank. Notice the wooden planks under your feet as you walk alongside the trolley tracks, and imagine what it might have been like when all of downtown Astoria was built on pilings over the river. The town you see as you look toward the hills was built entirely on fill, initially from ships' ballasts that were dumped overboard.

A word of caution: the wooden planks can become slippery when wet, and if you're riding a bike, mind the gaps between the boards.

① *Along the River*

Astoria's paved riverfront walk is 6.4 miles long, beginning at Smith Point to the west and continuing east past Thirty-ninth Street. Parking is available at the West Mooring Basin (Basin Street), Maritime Memorial Park (Bay Street), Columbia River Maritime Museum (Seventeenth Street), and the Sixth Street parking lot.

② *Astoria Riverfront Trolley*

A great way to get a quick introduction to Astoria, is to hop aboard the Astoria Riverfront Trolley. Ride as long as you like for one dollar, or pay two dollars and get on and off at your leisure all day long. It runs for three miles along the Columbia River while a conductor provides information on the area's history and attractions. A complete round trip takes about forty-five minutes. Hours vary from season to season, and are weather-dependent. Catch a ride at a marked stop (they are covered benches), or flag the trolley down at any location (wave your dollar!).

③ *Uniontown/West Mooring Basin*

This area of town, covering roughly thirty blocks, is known as "Uniontown," so called because of the Union Packing Company built here in 1881. A large Finnish population settled in this area, so it was also referred to as "Finn Town." The Uniontown-Alameda Historic District is roughly from Marine Drive and Alameda Avenue, and Hume and Hull avenues. Here you'll find a moorage for pleasure boats of all shapes and sizes, and offerings for fishing trips, ecotours, and river cruises.

At the foot of Basin Street is the Cannery Pier Hotel, built on the site of the 1896 Union Fishermen's Cooperative Packing Co. This upscale hotel looks very much like its predecessor.

④ *Astoria Bridge*

This 4.1 mile long bridge opened in 1966, and when built was the longest continuous truss span bridge in the world. It had a $1.50 toll until 1994, when the bridge was paid for and the toll removed. The bridge has more than two hundred feet of clearance on the Oregon side so large ships can pass beneath it in the shipping channel. One morning every October, traffic is restricted to one lane to accommodate the runners and walkers who participate in the 10K Great Columbia Crossing.

⑤ *Maritime Memorial Park* *(beneath the bridge at Bay Street)*

Maritime Memorial Park is dedicated to the memories of local people involved in the maritime industry. It also honors members of the U.S. Coast Guard who lost their lives while serving on the Columbia River.

Suomi Hall is the large white square building to the south. It was constructed in 1893 by the Finnish Temperance Society and was known as Temperance Hall. The Finnish Brotherhood purchased the building in 1934 and it is still used for their meetings.

⑥ *Site of Samuel Elmore Cannery* *(Marine Drive & Hume Street)*

In 1881, Samuel Elmore built a cannery on this site and out over the water on pilings. It was reputed to be one of the best equipped operations on the Pacific Coast. *(Photo of the cannery on page 69.)* In 1899, the Elmore Cannery joined with other canneries to form the Columbia River Packers Association (CRPA). The cannery continued to be successful until the 1940s when the salmon run declined sharply. When large schools of albacore were found off the coast of Oregon, CRPA added a tuna cannery to the site. In 1976 the cannery, then known as Bumble Bee Seafoods, ceased to can salmon and dealt strictly with tuna production until 1980 when it closed. The building was destroyed by fire in 1993.

Astoria Warehousing purchased the property and, for thirty-five years, received, stored, and labeled Alaska canned salmon, shipping it to all parts of the world. In 2019, Fort George Brewery purchased the 124,000 square-foot facility, expanding its brewing capabilities.

⑦ *Third Street*

The red brick building on the waterfront east of the Columbia House Condominiums was built in 1892 as the Astoria Wharf and Warehouse Co. to store tin plate and other accessories for manufacturing tin cans for salmon canning. It was occupied by seven different can companies until 1949, and has survived three major fires. Made from locally fired brick, the building's foundation goes down into the river bed. This is unusual because all other over-the-water structures were built on pilings. The granite keystone over the doorway and the granite door were taken from the custom house in east Astoria. It is the only surviving building to show this early "tin can" industry on the lower Columbia.

⑧ *Viewing Platform/Kinney Cannery* (*foot of Sixth Street*)

The viewing platform at the foot of Sixth Street is next to the site of the Kinney Cannery, the first cannery built in the downtown area in 1876. The building burned in 1894, and was rebuilt on its original supports in the early 1900s. It is rumored that large mounds of melted cans could be seen beneath the building from the fire. In 1989, the building was placed on the National Register of Historic Places. *In 2010, the building (housing the Cannery Cafe) was again destroyed by fire.*

⑨ *No. 10 Sixth Street*

A building on this site housed offices for the Columbia River Packers Association from 1915 to 1976. Subsequently, the historic building was revitalized, and converted to office and retail space. *In December 2010, the entire structure burned to the ground.*

⑩ *Ninth Street*

One block up from the river is Astor Street, once home to Astoria's red light district. The building at the corner of Ninth & Astor housed the only hotel in the commercial district to survive the 1922 fire. Retail and office space were on the first floor. The second floor housed the Douglas Hotel and a high class bordello. Most brothels were officially known as "female boarding houses" and appeared on early city maps from Seventh to Tenth streets.

In addition to brothels, this area was lined with gambling houses, opium dens, and taverns. In 1875, Astoria had twenty-seven saloons. A Portland newspaper described Astoria during the canning season as "the most wicked place on earth for its population."

During the salmon canning boom of the late 1800s, thousands of Chinese were hired to work in the canneries. A large number lived in this area on Astor and Bond Streets. Canneries were built side-by-side on the waterfront with Chinese bunkhouses directly behind and beneath the street.

⑪ *Twelfth Street*

This is where the river pilots dock their boats. Notice how small they are in comparison to the large vessels the pilot will board, like bulk carriers and container ships. The boat comes alongside the underway vessel and the pilot boards by climbing a rope ladder attached to the side.

(12) *Fourteenth Street Pier*

This is where ferries docked from 1921 until 1966, when the Astoria Bridge was completed. This is a public pier, which includes a radio speaker allowing visitors to hear live conversations of river pilots and the Coast Guard as they go about their work on the river.

(13) *Seventeenth Street Pier / Maritime Museum*

Astoria is the home port for the Coast Guard cutters *Alert* and *Steadfast*. When they aren't away enforcing federal fisheries and vessel safety laws, or assisting with homeland security or illegal immigration and contraband laws, they dock at the foot of Seventeenth Street. On occasion, one of the cutters will offer free guided tours. This is also where sternwheelers and other tour boats dock.

The Columbia River Maritime Museum has interactive exhibits for visitors of all ages. Included in the admission fee is a tour of the lightship *Columbia*. Before buoys lighted the way, this small vessel sat anchored at the entrance to the river, guiding ships safely into the channel.

(14) *Barbey Maritime Center/Scow Bay* (Eighteenth Street)

The abandoned 1924 train depot was historically restored in 2013, and is now the Barbey Maritime Center for Research and Industry. The center promotes maritime skills and the culture of Columbia River life, hosting classes and workshops in association with the Columbia River Maritime Museum.

Look across Marine Drive to the aquatic center. This area (between Eighteenth and Twenty-third streets) used to be underwater and was known as Scow Bay. Before a bridge was built in 1878 on what is now Exchange Street, residents traveled by boat between "Lower Astoria" to the west and "Upper Astoria" or "Uppertown" to the east.

(15) *Net Drying Loft* (Thirty-first Street)

The large red building out in the river was constructed in 1897 as a net drying and mending shed (or loft). Natural fiber nets, often made in fishermen's homes during the winters, needed to be dried between uses. Fishermen could navigate their boats under the building where a hoist would lift the nets to dry. The building sustained considerable damage during the Storm of 2007.

(16) *Custom House Reconstruction* (*Thirty-fourth on the south side of Leif Erickson Drive*)

John Adair was commissioned by President James Polk to establish a custom house in Astoria in 1849, the first west of the Rocky Mountains. The original building burned down and was rebuilt in 1852. This reconstructed model was built in 1991 to celebrate the bicentennial of the Customs Service.

(17) *East Mooring Basin* (*Thirty-sixth Street*)

The east mooring basin at the foot of Thirty-sixth Street is where you are likely to find hundreds of Steller and California sea lions sprawled on the docks and nearby rocks. When the wind is right, their barking can be heard all the way up the hill. Female sea lions can reach up to six feet and weigh about 200 pounds. Males can reach eight feet and weigh up to 880 pounds.

(18) *Historic Hanthorn Cannery* (*Thirty-ninth Street*)

The Hanthorn Cannery was originally built in 1875 and is the only remaining cannery building still standing. It has been renovated to accommodate a number of businesses, including a brew pub and coffee shop, both with outdoor seating.

While navigating the streets of Astoria, note that streets going up the hill are numerical, with intersecting streets in alphabetical order.

Self-Guided Tour
Downtown Astoria

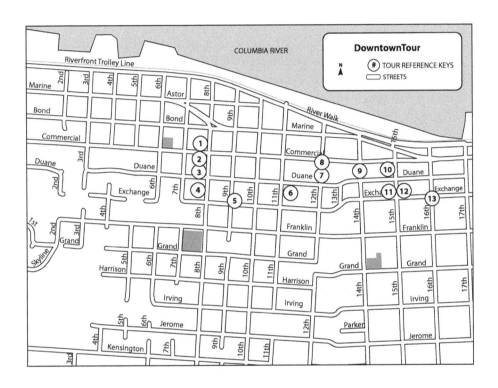

Circled numbers correspond to tour highlights
described on the following pages.

If you head for the hills you may encounter one or more of Astoria's "pigeon steps" or "clickety clacks." When Astoria's steep streets were constructed of wood, slats were nailed across the walkways to provide grip for pedestrians' shoes. When concrete sidewalks replaced the wooden walkways, the slats were recreated in concrete, or shallow steps were built. Good examples of pigeon steps and shallow steps can be found on Eighth, Tenth, and Eleventh streets (see pages 181, 183).

A good starting place for a historic tour of the downtown area is on Eighth Street, where you will find the post office, courthouse, and Flavel House museum. But, parking is scarce, so you might want to combine this tour with a partial riverfront tour.

Parking is available at the foot of Sixth Street, or at the Columbia River Maritime Museum. (The trolley stops at both locations.) If you arrived by cruise ship, another option is to take a bus from Pier 1 at the Port of Astoria.

To begin, make your way to Eighth & Commercial.

① *U.S. Post Office and Custom House* (*Commercial Street between Seventh & Eighth*)

The first post office west of the Rockies was established in Astoria in 1847, distributing mail throughout the region for forty cents. It ran from postmaster John Shively's home on Fifteenth Street between Exchange and Franklin. (A marble obelisk marks the spot).

The current post office, completed in 1933, is an American Renaissance style structure. It was erected on the site of the 1878 stone block building that housed the post office and custom house. Stones from that building were reportedly used in retaining walls throughout the city.

② *Clatsop County Courthouse* (*Commercial Street between Seventh & Eighth*)

County business was conducted in the town of Lexington, near present-day Warrenton, until 1854, when an election decided that Astoria would be the county seat. A two-story frame courthouse was built at the present courthouse site in 1855 and used until 1904, when construction began on a new building. Due to financial and contractual issues, it took four years to build. The current courthouse has been in use since 1908.

Eleventh Street "pigeon" steps, between Irving and Jerome.

At the west end of the courthouse, at the corner of Seventh Street, you will find a nine-foot diameter log cut from a 231-foot tall Douglas fir, placed there in 1937.

(3) ***The Old Jail (1914-1976)*** *(Behind the Courthouse on Duane Street between Seventh & Eighth)*

This was the county's third jail built on this site. Before wire screens were placed on the windows, it is rumored that friends of inmates would slip liquor to their incarcerated friends via long tubes, which they passed through the bars. The jail is the site of the opening scene in the movie, *The Goonies*, and is home to the Oregon Film Museum.

(4) ***Flavel House Museum*** *(Eighth Street, between Duane & Exchange)*

Built in 1885 by Captain George Flavel for his retirement, this Queen Anne style Victorian home and its period furnishings enable visitors to imagine life in Astoria at the turn of the last century. It has been operating as a museum since 1951. Captain Flavel became the first licensed Master Mariner to be granted a pilotage license for the Columbia River bar, and eventually became Astoria's first millionaire. Some say the Flavel house is haunted—lights turning off by themselves, phones ringing when not plugged in, drapes closing or opening by themselves. Purchase tickets at the Carriage House (Seventh & Exchange).

Cross Eighth Street and walk along Exchange Street to Ninth.

(5) ***Fire Boundary Marker*** *(Ninth & Exchange)*

At the northeast corner of Ninth and Exchange you will find a stone marker indicating the boundary of the 1922 fire that destroyed all of downtown Astoria. Notice as you walk through the downtown area that buildings were built in 1923 or later.

Walk east along Exchange, and turn left on Eleventh Street.

(6) ***Garden of Surging Waves*** *(Eleventh & Duane)*

This city park is designed to honor and celebrate the Chinese heritage of Astoria and the Lower Columbia River Basin. The Chinese played a significant role in the history of Astoria, working in the canneries, building the city's sewer system, constructing railroads connecting Astoria to Portland, and building the jetties at the mouth of the Columbia River. Many current residents are descended from the early families that built the city and provided labor for its first industries.

Walk along Duane to Twelfth Street.

To aid pedestrians, shallow steps (shown here on Eighth Street) replace traditional sidewalks on some of Astoria's steeper streets.

One block up, at the corner of Twelfth & Exchange, is the site of the old Astoria Theater. A marker indicates that Clark Gable began his acting career here in the summer of 1922. Gable was twenty-one when he joined the Astoria Players Stock Company.

⑦ *Hotel Elliott* (*Twelfth, between Duane & Commercial*)

Hotel Elliott opened in 1924 to accommodate post-fire construction workers. Large signs boasted the hotel's "Wonderful Beds." It remained in business until the 1960s when it began a slow decline. Chester Trabucco purchased the hotel and completely restored it in 2003. Bringing in top-of-the-line mattresses, he retained the "Wonderful Beds" sign.

Continue on Twelfth to Commercial Street.

⑧ *Liberty Theater* (*Twelfth & Commercial*)

Built in 1925, this restored theater is one of Oregon's best examples of a 1920s vaudeville/motion picture palace, with a Mediterranean exterior that continues inside with oil paintings of Venice by renowned regional artist Joseph Knowles. It originally offered silent movies and vaudeville acts. It is now a performing arts center.

Is there a ghost in here? It is said that a woman wearing Victorian era clothing is sometimes seen in the upstairs women's bathroom, visible when looking in the mirror. But when you turn around, she's gone.

Walk east on Commercial. Notice the narrow alleyway in the middle of the block. It's a by-product of an 1850s land feud between John Shively and John McClure. (*See page 42.*)

⑨ *Astor Hotel* (*Fourteenth Street between Commercial & Duane*)

This gothic-style hotel was initially built in 1923 with five stories and one hundred rooms. But since all but one hotel burned in the 1922 fire, three more floors were added, for a total of 150 rooms, making it the tallest building in Astoria. However, the hotel proved too large for the market and suffered financial trouble. It closed in 1968 and was vacant for eleven years. It was placed on the National Register of Historic Places in 1979, becoming low-income housing.

This is where, on Thanksgiving in 1948, Ed Parsons invented and developed cable television. He lived in an apartment of the hotel and discovered he could get a television signal from the roof. Using coaxial cable, he wired the signal across the street to Poole's Music Store, at the southwest corner of Duane and Fourteenth, making Poole's the first documented cable customer in the nation.

Continue east on Commercial to Fifteenth Street.

⑩ *Tidal Rock* *(Commercial & Fifteenth)*

Look over the railing and you will see the top of a large boulder. Look closely, and you can see a line that was chiseled into the rock in 1811, marking the high tide level. The rock's markings allowed a captain to determine how close to shore he could safely anchor his ship. The original riverbank was about one hundred feet south of here (up the hill).

Turn right on Fifteenth Street.

⑪ *Fort Astoria* *(Fifteenth & Exchange)*

A small park with partial replica of the fort is located at the site where John Jacob Astor's fur traders originally constructed their trading post. A mural recreates the vista from Astoria in 1813. There is also a monument (in English & Japanese) to Ranald MacDonald, grandson of Chinook Chief Comcomly. MacDonald was born at the fort, and in 1848 became Japan's first teacher of English. *Green diagonal lines on the street mark the outline of the original fort.*

A half-block up Fifteenth Street is a marble obelisk marking the location of the first post office west of the Rockies. The obelisk was placed there in 1955 by the Astoria Daughters of the American Revolution.

⑫ *Owens-Adair Apartments* *(Fifteenth & Exchange)*

On this site in 1880 the Sisters of Charity purchased the Arrigoni Hotel and, after a bit of remodeling, established St. Mary's Hospital, the first hospital in Astoria. It was added on to in 1895, and in 1905, a new building was constructed on the site that would later include a nursing school. This brick building was constructed in 1931. During its excavation, remnants of the Fort Astoria stockade were discovered. The building is named for a former Astoria resident, Bethenia Owens-Adair, thought to be Oregon's first woman surgeon.

Continue east on Exchange to Sixteenth Street.

⑬ *Heritage Museum* *(Sixteenth & Exchange)*

Built in 1904 as Astoria's City Hall, this building is now home to the Clatsop County Historical Society's regional museum. Explore the history of Clatsop County through temporary and permanent exhibits featuring Native Americans, early pioneers, immigrants, and local industries. The Society's Research Center and Archives are also here.

End Of Tour

To return to the riverfront, you can use the crosswalk at Sixteenth and Marine Drive. However, if traffic is heavy, it is recommended that you backtrack to Fourteenth Street, where you can safely cross Marine Drive via a traffic light.

As you approach Marine Drive from Fourteenth Street, notice Gimre's Shoes on the west side of the street. It is the oldest family-owned shoe store in the Western United States, having been in the Gimre family since 1892.

CHRONOLOGY

1500s	Spanish explorers visit the coast, leaving among their spilled cargo, beeswax that washed ashore and stories of buried treasure.
1775	First recorded sighting of the mouth of the Columbia by Spanish Captain Bruno de Heceta. He names it Rio San Rogue.
1778	Capt. James Cook makes landfall at Cape Foulweather and discovers fur wealth of Northwest Coast.
1788	Capt. Robert Gray trades with Indians in Tillamook Bay. After one of Gray's men is murdered, Gray names the bay "Murderer's Harbour." British Captain John Meares names Cape Disappointment.
1792	May 11, Capt. Robert Gray sails into the mouth of the Columbia, naming the river and giving the U. S. its first claim to the region. Capt. George Vancouver's expedition charts Columbia estuary.
1803	Louisiana Purchase extends United States to the Rocky Mountains.
1804	President Thomas Jefferson dispatches the Lewis & Clark Expedition.
1805	Lewis & Clark's overland party reaches the Pacific. They winter over at Fort Clatsop.
1811	The Pacific Fur Company establishes a trading company at Astoria. David Thompson of the North West Fur Company descends the Columbia River from Canada to Astoria.
1812	Overland Astorians discover South Pass in Wyoming, later route of the Oregon Trail. The U. S. declares war on Great Britain.
1813	Astoria is sold under duress to the British North West Company. They rename it Fort George for the King of England. The post continues to be known as Fort George for more than two decades.
1814	Treaty of Ghent resolves the War of 1812. First English woman, Jane Barnes, visits Fort George.

1818	The British surrender Fort George to the U.S., but remain on the scene.
	U.S. and Great Britain agree to "joint occupancy" of Oregon.
1821	The British North West and Hudson's Bay companies merge to become "the Company," known as the Hudson's Bay Company.
1824	U.S. and Russia agree to fifty degrees as southern boundary of Russian interests.
	Dr. John McLoughlin begins long tenure as Chief Factor for Hudson's Bay Company.
1825	Dr. John McLoughlin moves the center of operations of the Hudson's Bay Company to Fort Vancouver, in Washington.
1830	Chief Comcomly dies and "intermittent fever" rages through the Native American population.
1836	The first steamboat to enter the Columbia, the *Beaver*, arrives at Fort George.
1840	The number of Clatsop Indians is two hundred. In 1850, the number is down by half.
	The first white settlement on Clatsop Plains by Solomon H. Smith who, with Rev. J. H. Frost, establishes a Methodist mission.
1843	Land claims filed in Astoria by John McClure, John Shively, and A. E. Wilson.
1844	On June 22, Clatsop County is created by the Oregon provisional government.
	Oregon provisional government enacts a prohibition law preventing the sale and distillation of "ardent spirits" in Oregon.
	The first Oregon taxes are assessed.
	H. H. Hunt sets up the first sawmill on the Columbia River.
1845	An estimated 3,000 overland emigrants arrive in Oregon.

1846	There are ninety-five people on the census list for Clatsop County.
	The James Welch family moves to Astoria, the first permanent, European family there.
	The first shipwreck of major consequence (the U.S.S. *Shark*) takes place while attempting to cross the bar. A cannon from the wreckage is on display at the Heritage Museum.
	The boundary between the United States and Great Britain is settled at the 49th parallel.
1847	John Shively returns to Astoria from the East Coast with the commission of post master at Astoria, and opens the first post office west of the Rockies.
	B. C. Kindred starts the first passenger boat service from Astoria to upriver points.
1848	Ranald MacDonald is imprisoned in Nagasaki, and becomes Japan's first teacher of English.
	Gold is discovered in California. Immediately, a large number of new immigrants to Astoria head south.
	James Welch builds the first steam sawmill at about Ninth and Commercial.
1849	John Adair arrives with his commission as Customs Collector, the first on the West Coast.
	U. S. District Court meets in Clatsop County for the first time.
	Adam Van Dusen opens the first general store in Astoria.
	Oregon prohibition law is repealed by the territorial legislature.
1850	There are 462 people in Clatsop County.
	Congress passes the Donation Land Claim Act that attracts settlers by offering 320 acres for single men and 640 acres for married couples.
	Captain George Flavel arrives in Clatsop County. Within a few years, he has a monopoly on the bar pilot business.

1851	Tansy Point treaty negotiations are held with the Clatsop Indians, but are never ratified by Congress. In spite of this, the land is taken from the Clatsops and distributed by the U.S. government to "American" residents.
1852	640 acres of Indian land is set aside at Cape Disappointment for a future military reservation.
1853	The first church in Astoria, the Methodist Episcopal, is constructed on land donated by James Welch at Fifteenth and Franklin streets.
1854	Oregon's first public school district is established in Astoria. Astoria is named the seat of Clatsop County. The first unit of the future U.S. Coast Guard is stationed in the Pacific Northwest.
1856	The town of Astoria is incorporated. It has already gained the reputation of being one of the wildest towns on the West Coast. Cape Disappointment Lighthouse is constructed.
1859	February 14, Oregon becomes the Thirty-third state in the Union.
1860	There are 498 people in Clatsop County.
1861	The Civil War begins. Little effect is felt in Clatsop County, but sympathies of most lay with the North.
1862	Congress passes Homestead Act, giving settlers 160 acres of free land. Construction of Fort Canby begins.
1863	Construction of Fort Stevens begins.
1864	The first newspaper is published in Astoria, lasting for two years: the *Astoria Marine Gazette*. The last days of the Civil War are recorded in it.
1866	The first cannery on the Columbia River is built on the north shore of the Columbia River by the Hume Brothers.
1869	John West builds the first cannery in Clatsop County at Westport. The National Woman Suffrage Association and the American Woman Suffrage Association are formed.

1870	Population of Astoria is 639, and the county population is 1,255 (765 males and 490 females).
1871	The Pioneer & Historical Society is organized.
1873	The first mayor of Astoria is elected, W. F. Kippen.
	The *Astorian* newspaper begins operation under the direction of DeWitt Clinton Ireland.
	The Post Office/Custom House is constructed at its present site at Eighth and Commercial streets.
	The Astoria Chamber of Commerce is incorporated, the first in the Pacific Northwest.
	The first cannery in Astoria is incorporated in 1873 and built in January of 1874.
1875	There are seventeen salmon canneries in operation in the vicinity of Astoria on both sides of the river.
	Point Adams lighthouse is constructed.
1876	The Western Union completes a telegraph line to Astoria.
	Astoria has twenty-seven licensed saloons.
	The Kinney Cannery is the first cannery to be constructed in the downtown area.
1877	The first fire of consequence takes place in Astoria, burning the blocks around Fifth and Astor streets.
	Members of the Oregon & Washington Fish Propagation Company hold their first meeting in Astoria for the purpose of building fish hatcheries.
1878	A road across Scow Bay unites Upper and Lower Astoria.
	U. S. Life Saving Service established at Cape Disappointment.
1879	Columbia River Fishermen's Protective Union is formed.
1880	Bethenia Owens-Adair, a pioneer to the county in 1843, becomes one of the earliest women in the Northwest to earn a degree from a medical college.
	The Sisters of Charity open St. Mary's Hospital in Astoria.

1881	Construction of the Tillamook Lighthouse is completed.
	Samuel Elmore Cannery starts operating in Uniontown.
	There are thirty-five canneries on both sides of the Columbia River.
1882	U. S. Congress passes the Chinese Exclusion Act.
1883	Fire destroys a large portion of Astoria. It started at the Ferrell sawmill, about Fourteenth & Exchange, and spread to surrounding blocks.
	Astoria Street Railway Company is incorporated, with its cars pulled by horses.
1884	The first telephone exchange is started in Astoria.
1885	The first electric power is generated in Astoria at J. C. Trullinger's mill, and electric lights are installed.
	Flavel Mansion is built. Also constructed is the James Taylor house (on Sixteenth & Franklin).
	Work begins on the South Jetty.
1886	First logging railroad begins operating in Clatsop County.
	R. M. Brayne designs and builds the first ground pulp mill in Oregon at Young's River Falls.
1887	Finnish Temperance Society is organized and builds Suomi Hall in Uniontown.
1888	Road constructed from Young's Bay to Seaside.
	Astoria Street Railway Company begins streetcar service.
1889	John Chitwood is the first logger in Clatsop County to use a steam donkey.
1890	There are 10,016 people in the county.
	Astoria & South Coast Railway is built, running between Young's Bay and Seaside.
1892	Streetcars in Astoria are electrified.
	The first graduating class from Astoria High School (at McClure School) takes place.
	Congress authorizes *Columbia River Lightship No. 50*.
	Chinese Exclusion Act is extended for another ten years.

1893	December 1, the first legal hanging takes place in Astoria.
1894	The first Astoria Regatta takes place.
	Astoria has thirty-five rip-roaring saloons.
1895	Astoria & Columbia River Railroad begins construction from Astoria east along the Columbia River.
1896	A strike is called by the Fishermen's Union protesting the low price paid by canneries for fish. Violence erupts and the National Guard is called to quell the strike. Finnish and Scandinavian fishermen unite to gain control over their industry and establish the Union Fishermen's Cooperative Packing Company.
	The Louvre opens in Astoria, August Erickson's notorious saloon on Seventh and Astor streets.
	Construction of Fort Columbia begins.
	The North Pacific Brewery opens in Uppertown at Thirtieth & Marine Drive. It now houses the Firefighter's Museum.
1897	The first moving pictures in Astoria are shown.
	The Alaskan Gold Rush attracts many local residents.
1898	The first passenger train arrives in Astoria from Portland, promising a new era of prosperity.
	Pile driving for the Young's Bay Bridge is completed in December.
	North Head Lighthouse is constructed.
1899	The quarantine station at Knappton Cove opens.
1900	There are 13,765 people in Clatsop County and 8,831 in Astoria.
1903	Only seven canneries remain on the Columbia River.
1904	Astoria City Hall is constructed on the site of Fort George's burial ground at Sixteenth & Exchange.
	Astoria Socialist Club is formed.
	The first automobile arrives in Clatsop County, the Orient Motor Buckboard.
1908	A second courthouse is completed in Astoria, replacing the old wooden structure. It is still in use today.

1912	Woman's suffrage is approved in Oregon.
	Salmon trolling begins off the mouth of the Columbia River.
1914	Port of Astoria opens.
	Oregon legislation bans the manufacture and sale of alcoholic beverages.
1918	Washington/Oregon Columbia River Compact is formed by Congress to regulate commercial fishing activities on shared waters of the Columbia River.
1919	First gasoline tax in U. S. is authorized to fund Oregon's highways.
1920	Over 14,000 people live in Astoria.
1921	Ku Klux Klan organizes chapters and comes to Astoria.
	Captain Fritz Elfving begins a fifteen-car ferry service across the Columbia River.
	Astoria transfers ownership of 395 acres at Tongue Point to the government for a naval base.
1922	Compulsory Education Act is approved, requiring all children between the ages of eight and sixteen to attend public schools.
	In the early hours of December 8, thirty-two blocks of Astoria's downtown is destroyed by fire.
	Columbia River Highway is completed from Astoria to The Dalles, Oregon.
1924	Buses replace trolleys in Astoria.
	Hotel Elliott opens in downtown Astoria to house post-fire construction crews.
1925	A sterilization statute is adopted as state law in Oregon. Forced sterilization ends in 1983 with the abolishment of the Board of Social Protection.
	Compulsory School Act held unconstitutional.
	Liberty Theater opens in downtown Astoria.

1926	Fish wheels are abolished. The Astoria Column is completed. The Roosevelt Coast Military Highway is completed from Astoria to California. It was renamed the Oregon Coast Highway in 1931.
1930	Astoria's population drops to just over ten thousand.
1933	Voters repeal Oregon's constitutional prohibition amendment, and also ratify the Twenty-first Amendment to the U.S. Constitution, repealing national prohibition. Oregon Liquor Control Commission (OLCC) is formed.
1936	Astoria's municipal airport and seaplane ramp opens.
1938	Quarantine station at Knappton Cove closes.
1939	Tongue Point naval air station is formally dedicated.
1942	Executive Order 9066 authorizes removal of Japanese-Americans to internment camps on February 19. On June 21, a Japanese submarine fires seventeen rounds at Fort Stevens. Tire rationing goes into effect.
1943	Government repeals the Chinese Exclusion Act of 1882.
1947	War Department lists Fort Canby, Fort Columbia and Fort Stevens as surplus property.
1948	On Thanksgiving Day in Astoria, cable television is invented and developed by L. E. (Ed) Parsons. Coast Guard Station Cape Disappointment is created.
1952	Passenger train service in Clatsop County is discontinued.
1955	Community members build a replica of Fort Clatsop.
1959	Tongue Point naval base closes.
1962	Construction begins on the Astoria Bridge.
1964	Coast Guard Group/Air Station Astoria is established at Tongue Point naval station. They move to the Warrenton/Astoria airport in 1966.
1966	Bridge spanning the Columbia estuary is completed.
1974	Astoria Column is listed on the National Register of Historic Places.

1979	The last Oregon salmon cannery closes.
1983	Forced sterilization ends with the abolishment of the Board of Social Protection.
1984	Congress mandates that the Coast Guard establish a helicopter rescue swimmer program.
	The Goonies is filmed in Astoria.
1993	The Astoria Bridge is paid off and the tollbooth removed.
1998	Oregon State University Duncan Law Seafood Consumer Center opens.
1999	In May, the trolley begins making trips along the waterfront.
2004	July 10, a rededication ceremony is held for the restored Astoria Column with its beautified grounds.
2005	The Fort Clatsop replica burns to the ground on October 3.
	November 11, the five-day Lewis & Clark bicentennial celebration begins.
	December 10, construction of new Fort Clatsop replica begins.
	North Jetty repairs are made, using 58,000 tons of stone.
2006	South Jetty repair work begins, with stones averaging 17 tons.
	Dredging of the 103-mile Columbia River channel is authorized to a depth of forty-three feet to allow larger vessels access to Portland and other upriver ports.
2007	December 2nd and 3rd, a relentless storm pounds the coast of Oregon and Southwest Washington. Offshore buoys report eighty-foot waves, sustained winds are estimated at ninety to one hundred mph, with wind gusts upwards of 140 mph. All of Clatsop County loses power and phone service as hurricane force winds topple thousands of trees and severely damage many homes, storefronts, and other buildings. Clatsop County is cut off from the rest of the state as all roads leading in and out are blocked by fallen trees or flooding.
2014	May 17, grand opening of the Garden of Surging Waves at the corner of Eleventh & Duane streets, an interpretive park designed to honor Astoria's Chinese heritage.

E N D N O T E S

Astoria Bridge over the Columbia River.

(Note for Web site citations: Some Web sites may change the Web address for the citation or require a search from the home page to access the citation).

Chapter 1

1. "Northwest Explorers 1271-1791." www.oregonpioneers.com.

2. Fransen, Joean K. *Gray & Columbia's River*, pp 128-129.

3. "Wilkes, Charles (1798-1877): A Man With a Mission." www.historylink.org.

4. Penttila, Brian. *Columbia River: Astoria Odyssey*, p 6.

5. Swan, James G. *The Northwest Coast Or, Three Years' Residence in Washington Territory*, p 154.

6. Swan, pp 81-82.

7. Ziak, Rex. *In Full View*, inside cover.

8. Ziak, p 90.

9. Bell, Burnby. "A Few Notes on Chief Coboway." www.nps.gov/lewi.

Chapter 2

1. Ronda, James P. *Astoria & Empire*, p 112.

2. "Graveyard of the Pacific: The Shipwrecks of Vancouver Island." www.pacificshipwrecks.ca/English/.

3. Penttila, Brian. *Columbia River: Astoria Odyssey*, p 12.

4. "Diary of Wilson Price Hunt's Overland Journey to Astoria." www.xmission.com/~drudy/mtman/html/wphunt.

5. Swan, James G. *The Northwest Coast Or, Three Years' Residence in Washington Territory*, pp 225-226.

6. Swan, p 229.

7. Swan, p 230.

8. "Astor's Beechwood Mansion." www.astorsbeechwood.com/.

9. Dodds, Gordon B. *The American Northwest: A History of Oregon and Washington*, p 84.

10. "The Native Context and the Arrival of Other Peoples: Old World Contagions." The Oregon History Project. www.ohs.org/education/oregonhistory/narratives.

Chapter 3

1. "Oregon History-Overland to Oregon." The Oregon Blue Book, www.bluebook.state.or.us.

2. "Echoes of Oregon: A Brief History of the Oregon Territorial Period." Oregon State Archives, arcweb.sos.state.or.us/echoes/history.

3. Miller, Emma Gene. *Clatsop County, Oregon*, p 101.

4. Hannen, Tom. *The Illustrated Lower Columbia Handbook*, p 24.

5. Swan, James G. *The Northwest Coast Or, Three Years' Residence in Washington Territory*, p 53.

6. Swan, p 243.

7. Gray, Captain William P. "The Boy Mail Carrier of Astoria," *Cumtux, Vol. 1, No. 3*, pp 14-15.

8. Gray, p 16.

9. Miller, p 138.

10. Owens-Adair, Bethenia. *Dr. Owens-Adair: Some of Her Life Experiences*, p 260.

11. "Long Beach Peninsula Visitors Bureau." www.funbeach.com/attractions/lighthouse.

12. Miller, p 129.

13. Church, Stanley R., and Jim Dennon. "The Clatsop Indians," *Cumtux, Vol. 11, No. 1*, p 7.

14. Penttila, Bryan A. "So Much for Astoria: The Frontier Reality of Astor's Western Dream." *Cumtux, Vol. 22, No. 1*, p 11.

15. Swan, p 239.

Chapter 4

1. "Building Boom in Astoria." *Cumtux, Vol. 19, No. 1*, inside cover.

2. Miller, Emma Gene. *Clatsop County, Oregon*, p 144.

3. "The Sanitary Commission and Other Relief Agencies." www.civilwarhome.com/sanitarycommission.htm.

4. Owens-Adair, Bethenia. *Dr. Owens-Adair: Some of Her Life Experiences*, p 60.

5. Owens-Adair, p 61.

6. "The Sanitary Commission and Other Relief Agencies," p 4.

7. Martin, Irene Martin. *Legacy and Testament: The Story of Columbia River Gillnetters*, p 47.

8. *Astoria Daily Budget*, August 11, 1893.

9. Tetlow, Roger T. *The Astorian*, p 89.

10. Goodell, Rahles Blissett. "John A. & Elise Devlin: Pioneer Salmon Packers." *Cumtux, Vol. 19, No. 2*, p 2.

11. "Astoria's history along the tracks." www.homepage.mac.com/cearl/trolley.

12. "Samuel Elmore Cannery." National Historic Landmarks Program, www.nps.gov/history/nhl/.

13. "Samuel Elmore Cannery," 2.

14. Goodell, p 5.

15. Miller, May Spexarth. "Remembering Old Astoria: The Spexarth Family." *Cumtux, Vol. 18, No. 2*, p 4.

16. Tetlow, p 155.

17. Tetlow, p 164.

18. Friday, Chris. *Organizing Asian American Labor: The Pacific Coast Canned-Salmon Industry 1870-1942*, p 60.

19. "The First 400 Years From the 1500s to 1900." Clatsop County Historical Society, www.cumtux.org.

20. Pentilla, Brian. *Columbia River: Astoria Odyssey*, p 21.

21. Hankel, Evelyn G. "Early Astoria Breweries." *Cumtux, Vol. 9, No. 4*, p 21.

22. Miller, Emma Gene. p 132.

23. Alborn, Denise. "Shanghai Days in Astoria." *Cumtux, Vol. 9, No. 1*, p 12.

24. Trullinger, Thad S. "The 1883 Astoria Fire." *Cumtux, Vol. 9, No. 3*, p 23.

25. Trullinger, p 18.

26. "Astoria's history along the tracks", 11.

27. Dennon, Jim. "Astoria's Streetcars." *Cumtux, Vol. 9, No. 3*, p 31.

28. Johnson, Don. "In God We Trust," *Cumtux, Vol. 22, No. 4*, p 2.

29. Malcolm, Dawn. "Power and Endurance: The Building of the South Jetty." *Cumtux, Vol. 22, No. 4*, p 22.

30. Owens-Adair, p 420.

31. Owens-Adair, p 59.

32. Owens-Adair, p 68.

33. Reynolds, Dave. "Oregon Governor Apologizes For Eugenics' Misdeeds." *Inclusion Daily Express*, Dec 2, 2002.

34. "Women's Lib 1884." *Cumtux, Vol. 6, No. 3*, p 23.

Chapter 5

1. Cleveland, Alfred A. "Social and Economic History of Astoria." *Oregon Historical Society Quarterly, Vol. IV, No. 2*, p 149.

2. Miller, Emma Gene. *Clatsop County, Oregon*, p 134.

3. "The Orient Buckboard." *Cumtux, Vol. 1, No. 1*, p 23.

4. Miller, p 161.

5. Miller, p 148.

6. Bakke, Bill M. "Chronology of Salmon Decline: Columbia River, 1848 to Present." Native Fish Society, www.nativefishsociety.org/.

7. Churchill, Dorothy. "Sam Churchill." Oregon Cultural Heritage Commission, www.ochcom.org/Churchill.

8. Dodds, Gordon. *The American Northwest: A History of Oregon and Washington*, p 222.

9. Lovell, Robert S. "The War Years in Clatsop County." *Cumtux, Vol. 15, No. 3*, p 2.

10. "Oregon History—Mixed Blessings." The Oregon Blue Book, bluebook.state.or.us/.

11. McLain, Annie. "Unmasking the Oregon Klansman: The Ku Klux Klan in Astoria 1921-1925." http://Journals.iranscience.net:800/mcel.pacificu.edu/history/dept/students/theses2003/mclain/mclain.html.

12. Lucas, Peggy Chessman. "Chessman, Editor and Statesman." *Cumtux, Vol. 6 No. 4*, p 4.

13. Lovell, Bob. "Sherman Lovell and the Astoria Fire." *Cumtux, Vol. 5, No. 2*, p 33.

Chapter 6

1. Tetlow, Roger T. *The Astorian*, p 64.

2. Dennon, Jim. "Astoria's Streetcars." *Cumtux, Vol. 9, No. 3*, p 34.

3. Gragg, Randy. "Interpreting a pillar of the community." *The Sunday Oregonian*, Oct. 26, 2003.

4. Kennedy, Laura Couch. "Laura Couch's Famous Swim." *Cumtux, Vol. 4, No. 4*.

5. Dodds, Gordon. *The American Northwest: A History of Oregon and Washington*, p 226.

6. "Oregon History-World War II." The Oregon Blue Book, www.bluebook.state.or.us/.

7. Lovell, Robert S. "The War Years in Clatsop County." *Cumtux, Vol. 15, No. 3*, p 4.

8. Lovell, p 5.

9. "Shortage of Rubber Said Very Serious." *Evening Astorian Budget*, March 5, 1942.

10. "Cannery Help Plea Heard by Students." *Evening Astorian Budget*, September 8, 1942.

11. Barton, Richard. "Ed Parsons, An Oral History." The Cable Center Education and Information Resources, www.cablecenter.org/education/library/oralhistories.cfm.

12. Barton, p 3.

13. "Oregonian starts first cable television system." Clear Lines, Special Edition, July 1996, www.ccmtc.com/.

14. "Oregonian starts first cable television system."

15. Classen, Margaret L. "The Astoria CATV System." *Cumtux, Vol. 1, No. 4*, p 33.

Chapter 7

1. "Astoria Marine Construction Company." www.geocities.com/crodhull3/astoria.

2. "Station Cape Disappointment." www.uscg.mil/d13/units/gruastoria/.

3. Gragg, Randy. "Interpreting a pillar of the community." *The Sunday Oregonian*, October 26, 2003.

BIBLIOGRAPHY

Pillars from the Weinhard-Astoria Hotel, now in Shively Park, are all that remain of the luxury hotel.

Books

1. Dodds, Gordon B. *The American Northwest: A History of Oregon and Washington.* Illinois: The Forum Press, 1986.

2. Fransen, Joean K. *Gray & Columbia's River.* Seattle: Tabula Rosa Press, 1992.

3. Friday, Chris. *Organizing Asian American Labor: The Pacific Coast Canned-Salmon Industry 1870-1942.* Philadelphia: Temple University Press, 1994.

4. Hannen, Tom. *The Illustrated Lower Columbia Handbook.* 2001.

5. Martin, Irene. *Legacy and Testament: The Story of Columbia River Gillnetters.* Pullman: Washington State University Press, 1994.

6. Miller, Emma Gene. *Clatsop County, Oregon.* Portland: Binfords & Mort, 1958.

7. Owens-Adair, Bethenia. *Dr. Owens-Adair: Some of Her Life Experiences.* Mann & Beach Printers, 1906.

8. Penttila, Brian. *Columbia River: Astoria Odyssey.* Portland: Frank Amato Publications, 2003.

9. Ronda, James P. *Astoria & Empire*. Lincoln: University of Nebraska, 1990.

10. Ronda, James P. *Finding the West*. Albuquerque: University of New Mexico Press, 2001.

11. Swan, James G. *The Northwest Coast Or, Three Years' Residence in Washington Territory*. Seattle: University of Washington Press, 1992.

12. Tetlow, Roger T. *The Astorian*. Portland: Binford & Mort, 1975.

13. Ziak, Rex. *In Full View*. Astoria: Moffitt House Press, 2002.

Periodicals

1. Alborn, Denise. "Shanghai Days in Astoria." *Cumtux*, Vol. 9, No. 1.

2. "Building Boom in Astoria." *Cumtux*, Vol. 19, No. 1.

3. Church, Stanley R., and Jim Dennon. "The Clatsop Indians." *Cumtux*, Vol. 11, No. 1.

4. Classen, Margaret L. "The Astoria CATV System." *Cumtux*, Vol. 1, No. 4.

5. Cleveland, Alfred A. "Social and Economic History of Astoria." *Oregon Historical Society Quarterly*, Vol. IV, No. 2.

6. Dennon, Jim. "Astoria's Streetcars." *Cumtux*, Vol. 9, No. 3.

7. Goodell, Rahles Blissett. "John A. & Elise Devlin: Pioneer Salmon Packers." *Cumtux*, Vol. 19, No. 2.

8. Gray, Captain William P. "The Boy Mail Carrier of Astoria." *Cumtux*, Vol. 1, No. 3.

9. Hankel, Evelyn G. "Early Astoria Breweries." *Cumtux*, Vol. 9, No. 4.

10. Johnson, Don. "In God We Trust." *Cumtux*, Vol. 22, No. 4.

11. Kennedy, Laura Couch. "Laura Couch's Famous Swim." *Cumtux*, Vol. 4, No. 4.

12. Lucas, Peggy Chessman. "Chessman, Editor and Statesman." *Cumtux*, Vol. 6 No. 4.

13. Lovell, Robert S. "Sherman Lovell and the Astoria Fire." *Cumtux*, Vol. 5, No. 2.

14. Lovell, Robert S. "The War Years in Clatsop County." *Cumtux*, Vol. 15, No. 3.

15. Malcolm, Dawn. "Power and Endurance: The Building of the South Jetty." *Cumtux*, Vol. 22, No. 4.

16. Miller, May Spexarth. "Remembering Old Astoria: The Spexarth Family." *Cumtux*, Vol. 18, No. 2.

17. Penttila, Bryan A. "So Much for Astoria: The Frontier Reality of Astor's Western Dream." *Cumtux*, Vol. 22, No. 1.

18. "The Orient Buckboard." *Cumtux*, Vol. 1, No. 1.

19. Trullinger, Thad S. "The 1883 Astoria Fire." *Cumtux*, Vol. 9, No. 3.

20. "Women's Lib 1884." *Cumtux*, Vol. 6, No. 3.

Newspapers

1. "Cannery Help Plea Heard by Students." *Evening Astorian Budget*, September 8, 1942.

2. Gragg, Randy. "Interpreting a pillar of the community." *The Sunday Oregonian*, Oct. 26, 2003.

3. Reynolds, Dave. "Oregon Governor Apologizes For Eugenics' Misdeeds." *Inclusion Daily Express*, Dec. 2, 2002.

4. "Shortage of Rubber Said Very Serious." *Evening Astorian Budget*, March 5, 1942.

Web Sites

(Note: Some Web sites may change the Web address for the citation or require a search from the home page to access the citation).

1. "Astoria Marine Construction Company." (Written by Tom Dyer; personal web site) www.geocities.com/crodhull3/astoria.

2. "Astoria's History Along the Tracks." (Web site of Astoria Riverfront Trolley Association) www.homepage.mac.com/cearl/trolley.

3. "Beechwood History." (Web site of Astors' Beechwood Mansion, a living history museum) www.astorsbeechwood.com.

4. "Chronology of Salmon Decline: Columbia River, 1848 to Present." (Written by Bill M. Bakke; web site of Native Fish Society, a non-profit dedicated to conservation of wild fish in the Pacific Northwest) www.nativefishsociety.org.

5. "Ed Parsons, An Oral History." www.cablecenter.org/education/library/oralhistories.cfm. (Written by Richard Barton; web site of The Cable Center, a non-profit providing education and history related to the cable industry).

6. "A Few Notes on Chief Coboway." www.nps.gov/lewi. (Written by Burnby Bell; National Park Service web site for Lewis & Clark National Historical Park).

7. "Sam Churchill." www.ochcom.org/churchill. (Written by Dorothy Churchill; web site of Oregon Cultural Heritage Commission, a non-profit supporting Oregon arts, culture, and history).

8. "Diary of Wilson Price Hunt's Overland Journey to Astoria." (Personal web site) www.xmission.com/~drudy/mtman/html/wphunt.

9. "Echoes of Oregon: A Brief History of the Oregon Territorial Period." (Web exhibit from the Oregon State Archives) arcweb.sos.state. or.us/echoes/history.

10. "Graveyard of the Pacific: The Shipwrecks of Vancouver Island." (Web site of Maritime Museum of British Columbia) www. pacificshipwrecks.ca/English.

11. "Long Beach Peninsula Visitors Bureau."(Tourism web site) www. funbeach.com/attractions/lighthouse.

12. "Unmasking the Oregon Klansman: The Ku Klux Klan in Astoria 1921-1925." (Written by Annie McLain; student thesis at Pacific University) http://Journals.iranscience.net:800/mcel.pacificu.edu/ history/dept/students/theses2003/mclain/mclain.html.

13. "Northwest Explorers 1271-1791." (Compiled by Stephenie Flora; personal web site) www.oregonpioneers.com.

14. "Oregon History—Mixed Blessings." (Written by Stephen Dow Beckham; web site of Oregon State Archives) www.bluebook.state. or.us/.

15. "Oregon History—Overland to Oregon." (Written by Stephen Dow Beckham; web site of Oregon State Archives) www.bluebook.state. or.us/.

16. "Oregon History—World War II." (Written by Stephen Dow Beckham; web site of Oregon State Archives) www.bluebook.state. or.us/.

17. "Oregonian Starts First Cable Television System." (Web site of Clear Creek Telephone & Television, Clear Lines newsletter, July 1996) www.ccmtc.com.

18. "Port of Longview." (Official web site) www.portoflongview.com.

19. "Samuel Elmore Cannery." (National Historic Landmarks Program; National Park Service web site) www.nps.gov/history/nhl.

20. "Station Cape Disappointment." (U.S. Coast Guard web site) www.uscg.mil/d13/units/gruastoria.

21. "The First 400 Years From the 1500s to 1900." (Clatsop County Historical Society web site) www.cumtux.org.

22. "The Native Context and the Arrival of Other Peoples: Old World Contagions." (Written by William G. Robbins for the Oregon History Project; web site of the Oregon Historical Society) www.ohs.org/education/oregonhistory/narratives.

23. "The Prohibition Years: Bootleggers and Imagination." (Web exhibit from the Oregon State Archives) arcweb.sos.state.or.us/.

24. "The Sanitary Commission and Other Relief Agencies." (Excerpt from *The Photographic History of the Civil War*, written by Holland Thompson; web site maintained by Dick Weeks) www.civilwarhome.com/sanitarycommission.htm.

25. "Wilkes, Charles (1798-1877): A Man With A Mission." (Written by Junius Rochester, History Link Essay 5226; web site of HistoryLink.org, the Online Encyclopedia of Washington State History) www.historylink.org/.

ACKNOWLEDGMENTS

One of the most difficult aspects of writing a history is to decipher the contradictory information uncovered during the research process. As I discovered differing accounts of events, I did my best to determine the truth.

In that regard, I give a huge thank you to Liisa Penner, Archivist at Clatsop County Historical Society. Her knowledge of Astoria's history is unsurpassed. Her assistance was paramount in my quest for accuracy.

I would like to recognize the history buffs who researched and wrote the fascinating articles for *Cumtux*, the quarterly publication of Clatsop County Historical Society, from which I gleaned much of the material for this book.

Deep gratitude to my husband Dan who was there every step of the way, offering creative ideas and invaluable editorial comments.

To my daughters, Darcy and Megan, I offer my thanks for their encouragement and support.

Special thanks to my friend Bill Hubbard, whose tenacity and love of history provided the impetus I needed to begin the writing process in the first place, and who assisted me in research.

My appreciation to the following for their expertise and/or assistance: Nancy Bell Anderson, Dick Basch, McAndrew Burns, Barbara Cook, Captain Robert Johnson, Rosemary Johnson, LTJG Amy Sandbothe USCG, Lisa Studts, Dan Supple, Jane Tucker, Patrick Webb.

To my friend Bill W. Dodge for creating the wonderful painting for the cover. To find more of Bill's paintings, visit his web site at www.billwdodge.com.

To the following for the use of their photographs:

Clatsop County Historical Society

Larry Kellis Photography

Northwestern University Library

Salem Public Library Historic Photograph Collections

Oregon Department of Transportation

Oregon State Archives

Cannery Pier Hotel

Library of Congress

U.S. Coast Guard

U.S. Army Corps of Engineers

Ray Hakala

Steve Zalewski

To Bob Regan for creating the tour maps.

My appreciation to Cheryl Towers, Christine Cooper, and Harold Maguire for editing and layout assistance.

Karen L. Leedom

AUTHOR

Karen Leedom is a writer who lived in Astoria for almost twenty years. Her love of history and fondness for Astoria prompted her to write this book. Karen has since moved from the area, but will forever cherish the years she resided in this unique northwest corner of Oregon.

INDEX

Page numbers in italics refer to maps and photographs.

Adair, John, 42, *43*, 46, 48, 52, 178, 189
Adair, John, Jr., 104
Adams, William, 46
A. Guthrie and Company, 132
Albatross (ship), 20
Anti-Saloon League, 104
Astor Fur Company, 132
Astor Hotel, 142, 184
Astor, John Jacob, 1, 20, 22, 26, 185-186
Astor Street Opry Company, 82
Astoria, 1811, *19*; c. 1841, *27*; c. 1848, *33*; c. 1867, *61*; c. 1880s, *66-67*; (map) c. 1900, *44-45*; c. 1905, *109*; c. 1912, *i*; c. 1914 from Uppertown, *102-103*; c. 1915, *110-111*; 2007, *1, 163, 173*
Astoria & Columbia River Railroad, 94, 193
Astoria & South Coast Railway, 94, 192
Astoria Aquatic Center, 147, 172, 177
Astoria Bridge (Astoria-Megler Bridge), construction & development, 118, 150, *151*, 195, 196; Tapiola Park model, 158, *159*, 168; tour, 174
Astoria Column, 28-29, 42, 104, *129*, 131-133, 156, 167, 195-196
Astoria Electric Company, 97
Astoria Evening Budget (newspaper), 98, 123, 126
Astoria Law Enforcement League, 122
Astoria Marine Construction Company, 138, 144
Astoria Marine Gazette (newspaper), 190
Astoria Progressive Commercial Commission, 131
Astoria Socialist Club, 114, *115*, 193
Astoria Soda Works, *106*, 106
Astoria Transit Company, 130
Astoria Warehousing, 175
Astoria-Warrenton Area Chamber of Commerce, 152, 156, 170, 191
Astoria Wharf and Warehouse Co., 175
Automobile (first in county), 116, 193
Badollet & Company Cannery, 68
Baker, Elna Christansen, 132
Baker, George L., 132
Baker's Bay (WA), 100
Bank of Commerce, 127
Bar pilot(s), 48-52, 148-150, 189
Barbey Maritime Center, 177
Barnes, Jane, 25, 188
Barnett, John, 111
Battle of Woody Point (Canada), 22
Beaver (ship), 24, 188
Benji the Hunted (movie), 151
Bennes and Herzog (architects), 131
Birnie, James, 27, 34
Board of Social Protection, 104, 194, 196
Booth & Company Cannery, 68

Bornstein Seafoods, Inc., 155
Brayne, R. M., 96, 166, 192
Broughton, William, 8, 166
Brown, Captain Hiram, 36
Budd, Ralph, 132
Bumble Bee Seafoods, 69, 137, 175
Burial canoe (Chinook), *9*, 12, 28, 30
Burlington Northern Railroad, 154, 160
Butterfly fleet. *See* fishing
Cable television, 141-142, 185, 195
Canneries, decline of 118, 137, 144; employment in 70-74, *71*, 176; history of 36, 68-70, 113, 175, 176, 178, 190, 192, 193, 196; strike of 1896, 100-102. *See also* by name
Cannery Pier Hotel, *101*, 102, 174, 210
Cape Disappointment, military history, 52, 57, 62-63, 190; naming, 7, 187; United States Coast Guard, 92-93, 146, *147*, 191, 195
Cape Disappointment Lighthouse, 52-55, *54*, 93, 190
Cape Disappointment State Park, 165
Cape Hancock, 7
Catalina flying boats, 138
Cathedral Tree Trail, 38, 42
Catherine the Great, 4
Celiast. *See* Smith, Celiast (Helen)
Centennial of 1911, 110-112, *112-113*, 170
Centennial Park, 111, *114*. *See also* Shively Park
Chatham (ship), 8
Chessman, Merle, 137
Chinese, 72-75, *71*, 138, 176, 192, 195
Chinese Exclusion Act, 70-71, *72*, 192, 195
Chinese tongs, 74
Chinook Indians, customs, *9*, 12, 28, 30, 165; disease, 29; history, 1, 10, *11*, 144-145; housing, 12-13, *13*, 14; religion 14; relocation, 57-58, 145-146; trade, 11, 15, 20, 23; transportation, 13. *See also* Chief Comcomly
Chinook Point, 63
Chitwood, John, 96, 192
Churches, 56, 59, 85-88, 104, 115-116, 122, 190, 199. *See also* by name
Civilian Conservation Corp (CCC), 137
Civil War, 63, 103, 116, 120-121, 164, 190
Clark, Alfred, 81
Clatsop Community College, 131
Clatsop County, courthouse, *57*, 58-59, 180, 189; development of, 35-36, 58-59, 67, 168, 185, 188-189, 193; economy, 36, 64, 96. 119. 136. 189. 192; flu epidemic, 98; old jail, 182; Ku Klux Klan in, 121-124; map, *vi*; movie locations, 152; suffrage movement, 106-108; temperance movement, 104-106; World War I, 120; World War II, 138-140

Clatsop County Heritage Museum, 26, 80, 110, 168, 185, 189

Clatsop County Historical Society, 26, 30, 152

Clatsop Indians, 15-18, *29*, 34, 57, 188, 190, 199

Clatsop Mill Company, 160, *161*

Clatsop-Nehalem Confederated Tribe, 145

"Clickety Clacks" (steps), 182

Coboway (Clatsop Chief), 10, 16, 35. *See also* Smith, Celiast (Helen)

Columbia Rediviva (ship), *3*, 6, 9

Columbia River, Chinook homeland, 144; commerce, 38, *40-41*, 42, 62, 64, *65*, 66-70, *69*, 113, 118-119, 120-121, 141, 158-160, 188, 190, 192-194; defense of, 62, 120, 137; early exploration of, 5, 7-10, 15, 20-22, 27-28, 187; history of, 8; navigation, *3*, 28, 42, 54, *89*, 88-90, 91-92, 148-150, 196; swimming, 133-134; tourism/tours, 1-2, *163*, *173*, *179*; transportation, 48, 50, 97-98, 116, *117*, *143*, 150, 188, 194, *197*; United States Coast Guard, 146

Columbia River Fishermen's Protective Union, 66, 191

Columbia River Maritime Museum, 92, 158, 168, 174, 177, 180

Columbia River No. 50 (lightship), *91*,92

Columbia River No. 604 (lightship), *91*, 92

Columbia River Packers Association, 70, 100, 137, 175

Columbia River Quarantine Station (Knappton Cove). *See* United States Quarantine Station

Comcomly (Chinook Chief), 10, 15, 21-23, 26, 28-30, 63, 186, 188

Come See the Paradise (movie), 151

Commander's House Museum, 165

Compulsory Education Act, 122-123, 194

Cook, James, 5

Cornelisen, Jack, 127

Corno, Paul, 50

Couch, Laura, 133-134

Courthouse, 57, 59, 102, 110, 151, 180, 193

Cox, Ross, 24, 38

Coxcomb Hill, 111, 120, 123, 131, 142, 167

Craniometry, 30

Crimping. *See* shanghaiing

Crown Zellerbach Corporation, 96

Cruise ships, 1-2, 81, 85, 159

Custom House, 42, 46, *49*, 102, 176, 178, 180, 191

"Daddy trains", 94

Daily Astorian, The (newspaper), 70, 75, *77*, 90, 97

de Fuca, Juan, 4, 9

de Heceta, Bruno, 4, 7, 187

Demers, Father Modeste, 85

Depression years, 133, 136-137

Desdemona (ship), 90

Desdemona Sands Lighthouse, 90

Dever, Lem, 122

Discovery (ship), 7

Donation Land Claim Act, 34, 56, 189

Dorion, Marie and Pierre, 21

Downtown Astoria, canneries 68, 144, 175, 176, 191; celebrations, 110, 120, 134, 170; fires, 82, *83*, 124, 130, 194; tours of, 163, 173, 179, *179*

Duncan Law Seafood Consumer Center, 155, 196

Duniway, Abigail Scott, 108

East Mooring Basin, 178

Elfving, Fritz, 117-118, 194

"Ellis Island of the Columbia", 97-98, *99*, 172, 193, 195. *See* United States Quarantine Station

Erickson, August, 42, 78-80, 193

Evans, Dan, 150

Executive Order 9066, 195

Explorer(s), 2, 4, 10, 16, 20, 160, 187, 196, 197. *See also* by individual name

Ferries, 117-118, 138, 177, 194

Finland, 67, 113-116

Finnish Apostolic Lutheran Church, *87*, 86

Finnish Brotherhood, 106, 175

Finnish immigrants, 103, 113-116

Finnish Socialist Federation, 114, 116

Finnish Temperance Society, 106, 175, 192

Finn Town, 68, 174

Fire Boundary Marker, 182

Fire of 1883, 82, *83*, 124

Fire of 1922, 124-127, *124-125*

Fishing, butterfly fleet, *65*, 66; Chinese exclusion, 71; Chinook rights, 145; declining, 70, 118; fish traps, 64, 100; fish wheels, 64, 118, 195; gillnet, 64, 66, 100, 139; horse seines, 64, 118, *119*; record catches, 141. *See also* Union Fisherman's Net Drying Loft

Fish propagation, 191

Flavel, George, 48, *50*, 50, *51*, 86, 150, 168, 182, 189

Flavel House Museum, 158, 168-169, *171*, 182

Fort Astoria, 22-24, *25*, 31, 164, 170, 185

Fort Canby, 54, 63, 138, 146, 165, 190, 195

Fort Clatsop, 15-16, *17*, 20, 159, 164, 169, 187, 195, 196

Fort Columbia, 10, 63, 164-165, 193, 195

Fort Columbia State Park, 164-165

Fort George, 25-27, 30, *33*, 34, 187, 188, 193

Fort Stevens (& State Park), 10, *13*, 14, 16, 63, 86, 89, 120, *121*, 127, 138-140, 164, 190, 195

Fort to Sea Trail, 164

Fort Vancouver, 27-28, 35, 85, 188

Free Willy (movie), 151-152

Friends of the Astoria Column, 156

Frost, Rev. John H., 34

14th Street Pier, 117, 177

Fur trading, 1, 4-5, 8, 19-20, 26-27

Gable, Clark, 183

Gairdner, Meredith, 29-30

Gale, James Newton, 75

Garden of Surging Waves, 75, 182, 196

Geer, Theodore T., 107

Gillnet. *See* fishing
Gimre's Shoes, 186
Goble (WA), 94
Golden Trail, The, 36
Goonies, The (movie), 151-152, *153*, 182, 196
Grant, Bridget, *81*, 82
Grant, Ulysses S., 58, 78, 160
Gray, Robert, 3, 6-7, 131-132, 159-160, 187
Gray, William P., 46
Great Northern Railroad, 131-133
Halloran, J. F., 78
Hammond, Andrew B., 94, 111, 120
Hammond Lumber Company, 111
Hammond Mill, 119
Hanthorn Cannery, 154, 178
Hanthorn's Addition, 110
Hapgood, Andrew, 68
Harbor (Astoria), *53*
Harley, Francis Clay, 120
Harvest Queen (steamer), 100
Hatfield, Mark, 150
Hayes, Rutherford B., 78
Helicopter rescue swimmer program, 146, 196
Henderson, H.L., 112
Heritage Museum, 185
Hill, George, 104
Hill, Legrand, 103
"Hindu Alley", 119
Hobson, John, 36, 64, 103
Hobson, William, 36
Homestead Act, 62, 190
Horse seines. *See* fishing
Hotel Elliott, 130, *157*, 158, 184, 194
Hudson's Bay Company, 26-30, 34-35, 48, 58, 188
Hug, Wally, 133
Hume, George, 68, 70, 152, 174, 190
Humphreys, Mr. & Mrs. Charles, 136
Hunt, H. H., 38, 188
Hunt, Wilson Price, 21, 23
Indian Reorganization Act, 145
Industry (ship), 93
Into the Wild (movie), 151, 152
Ireland, DeWitt Clinton (D.C.), 75, *77*, 78, 191
Ireland, Olive, 78
"Iron Chinks", 74
Isaac Todd (ship), 25
Jail(s), 80, 151, 182
Japanese, 31, 119, 138, 139, 140, 185, 195
Jefferson Davis (ship), 52
Jetties, 88-90, *89*, 137, 184, 192, 196
Joseph Barrell & Company, 5
Joseph Lane (ship), 52
Kalama (WA), 94
Kathlamet tribe, 58
Kindergarten Cop (movie), 152
Kendrick, John, 5-6, 8
Kindred, B.C., 48, 189

Kinney Cannery, 68, 176, 191
Kippen, W.F., 191
Kiwanis Club, 126
Knappton Cove Quarantine Station. *See* United States Quarantine Station
Knappton, port of, *99*
Knights of Columbus, 122
Knowles, Joseph, 131, 168, 184-185
Korean War, 144
Kratz, O. A., 130
KRSC-TV, 142
Ku Klux Klan, 122-124, *123*, 194
Lady Washington (ship), 6, 8
Lausanne (ship), 34
Law, Duncan, 156, 196
League of Oregon Cities Award for Excellence, 158, 169
Leathers Shipbuilding, 120
Legislative Commission on Indian Services, 145
Leick, C. W., 54
Lewis and Clark Bicentennial, 1, 16, 160, 196
Lewis and Clark Corps of Discovery, 1, 14-16, *17*, 20, 55, 132, 156, 164-166
Lewis and Clark Interpretive Center, 55, 165-166
Liberty Theater, 131, *152*, 156, 168, 184, 194
Lighthouse(s), 52-55, 63, 90, 92-93, 190-193, 199. *See also* by name
Lighthouse Service, 52, 92
Lightships, 91-92, 158, 168, 177, 192
Linn, Lewis, 34
Litchfield, Electus D., 132
Logging, *39-41*, 94, 95-96, 118-119, 192
Louvre, The, *78-80*, 193
Lovell, Robert, 140, 201, 204
Lovell, Sherman, 126, 201, 204
Lower Astoria, 42-43, 46, 84, 177, 191
Lutheran church (Uppertown), 86, *88*
Lynch, Paddy, 81-82
MacDonald, Archibald, 27, 30
MacDonald, Raven, 30
MacDonald, Ranald, 30-31, 186, 189
Maritime Memorial Park, 175
McClure, John, 35, 42-43, *44*, 58, 188, 192
McDougall, Duncan, 21-23, 25
McDougall, Ilchee, 23
McLoughlin, John, 27-28, 188
McTavish, Donald, 25-26
McTavish, John George, 25
Meares, John, 7, 187
Methodist church (1882), 59, 85, *86*
McEachern (shipyard), 120
Michel, Jennie, *29*
Miller, May Spexarth, 72, 199
Missionaries, 34
Morning Astorian (newspaper), 79-80, 110-112, 122, 127
Mott, James, 137

Movies, 126, 131, 151-152, 154, 158, 182, 184. *See also* by title

Munson, Joel, 92-93

National Community Television Association, 142

National Motor Life Boat School, 146

National Register of Historic Places, 69, 100, 156, 170, 172, 176, 184, 196

National Trust for Historic Preservation, 157-158

Native Americans, 111, *112-113*, 145. *See also* by tribal and individual names

Nehalem (tribe), 94

Net Drying Loft, *65*, 178

Nez Perce tribe, 111, *112-113*

Northern Pacific Railroad, 94

North Head Lighthouse, 54-55, *55*, 193

North Pacific Brewery, 78, *79*, 170, 193

North West Fur Company, 20, 187

Norton, Gale, 145

Oberst, Mary, 158

Occident Hotel, *56*, 78, 127

Octopus. See Tourist No. 2

Old Number 300 (trolley), 154, *155*

Olney, Cyrus, 43, 166

Oregon City Enterprise (newspaper), 75, *77*

Oregon City (OR), 48, 75, 77, 97

Oregon Coast Highway, 117, 195

Oregon Film Museum, 182

Oregon Liquor Control Commission, 195

Oregon National Guard, 102

Oregon Recreation and Park Association Design Award, 159, 169

Oregon State University Duncan Law Seafood Consumer Center, 156, 196

Oregon Suffrage Association, 108

Oregon Trail, 34, 187

Oregon and Washington Fish Propagation Company, 191

Orient Motor Buckboard, 116, 193

Owens-Adair, Bethenia, 36, 64, 102-104, *105*, 185, 191, 198, 199, 203

Owens-Adair Apartments, 78, 185

Pacific Fur Company, 20-21, *25*, 34, 38, 187

Panama Canal, 112-113

Parker, P. W., 78

Parker, W. W., 58, 105

Parker, Mrs. W. W., 105

Parsons, Ed, 141-142, 185, 202, 205

Penner, Liisa, 98

Perry, Matthew C., 31

Pierce, Walter, 122, 132

Pigeon steps, *181*, 182

Pilot boats, 52, *53*, 148, *149*

Point Adams, 28, 34, 62, 63

Point Adams Lighthouse, 90, 191

Poole's Music Store, 142, 184

Portland (OR), Astoria Column plans, 131-132; exile to *71*, 72, 84, 140; Ku Klux Klan membership 123; 1922 fire relief, 127; quarantine office, 100; port, 113, 150, 160-161, 196; shanghaiing, 81-81; travel between, 2, 85, 94-95, *95*, 193; ship repairs/shipyard, 92, 138

Powers, T. P., 46

Preble (naval ship), 31

Prohibition, 78-80, 104-106, 122, 188, 189, 195

Pulp mill(s), 96, 166, 192

Pusterla, Attilio, 132-133

Quarantine station. *See* United States Quarantine Station

Quinault Indian Reservation, 145-146

Railroads, building of, 70, *89*, 90, 95, 120; Great Depression, 136; immigration, 98, 116; logging, *94*, 96, 192; to/from Portland, 94-95, *95*, 116, 193. *See also* "daddy trains", railroads by name

Red light district, 78, 176

Reed, Jim, 133

Reeves, S.C., 48

Regatta, 24, 74, 78, 133-135, *134-135*, 193

Reliance Electrical Works, 116

Relocation (internment) of Japanese residents, 140, 195. *See also* Executive Order 9066

Ring II, The (movie), 152

River pilots, 28, 30, 48, 118, 148, *149*, 150, 177

Rodgers Shipbuilding, 120

Roosevelt Coast Military Highway, 116, 195

Rossiter, Fred, 133

Rotary Club, 31, 126

Russian revolution, 116

Sacagawea, 15

Saloon(s), 56, 59, 80, 193

Samuel Elmore Cannery, 69, 137, 155, 175, 192

Sanitary Commission, 63-64, 103, 199

Santiago (ship), 4

Sawmill(s), 38, 58-59, 82, 84, 96, 188, 189, 192. *See also* by name

Schnitzer, Jordan, 156

Scow Bay, 42, 46, *47*, 84, 177, 191

Seaside (OR), 84, 94-95, 117, 133, 192

Seattle (WA), 95, 110, 113, 142

Seines (fishing), 64, 118-119, *119*

Seventeenth Street Pier, 168, 177

Shallow steps, 180, *183*

Shanghaiing, 80, 81, *81*, 82

Shepardson, Alfred, 80

Sherman, William Tecumseh, 78

Shipyards, 120, 138

Shively, John, 35-36, *37*, 42-43, *44*, 180, 188-189

Shively Park, 111, 114, *124*, 126, 170, *203. See also* Centennial Park

Short Circuit (movie), 152

Shortess, Robert, 36, 56

Shubrick (lighthouse tender), 54

Sisters of Charity, 76, 185, 191

Slavery, 10, 12, 28

Smith, Celiast (Helen), *35*

Smith Point, 36, 120

Smith, Samuel, 36

Smith, Solomon H., 34-35, *35*, 48, 188
Socialism, 113-116
Socialist Finns, 114-116
South Pass, 34, 187
St. Mary, Star of the Sea, 85, *87*
St. Mary's Hospital, 76, *77*, 185, 191
Staples Motor Company, 127
Staples, Norris, 127
Steam donkey (engine), 96, *97*, 192
Stork, Cpl. Robert, 140
Strike of 1896, 100
Stuart, David, 21
Stuart, Robert, 34
Suffrage movement. *See* women's rights
Sunday Market, 160, 170
Suomi Hall, 106, 175, 192
Surf rescue, *93*
Swan, James G., 12, 59, 197-198
Tacoma (WA), 81, 95
Talapus (wolf-spirit), 14
Tansy Treaty, 57
Tapiola Park, 158, *159*, 168
Tapiola Park Playground, 168
Teenage Mutant Ninja Turtles III (movie), 151
Temperance movement, 103, 104-106, 108, 175, 192
T. F. Oaks (ship), 81
Thompson, David, 20, 22, 187
Thorn, Jonathan, 20
Tidal Rock, 185
Tillamook Head, 10
Tillamook, Oregon, 138
Tillamook tribe, 58, 187, 192
Tongue Point, Clatsops, 10; Lewis & Clark, 15; Naval Air Station, 138, *139*, 144, 146, 195; naval base, 120; trans-Columbia swim, 134; Tongue Point Job Corps Center, 144
Tonquin (ship), 20-22, *23*, 34
Tourist, The (ferry), 117
Tourist No. 2 (ferry/mine layer), *117*, 117, 138
Tourist No. 3 (ferry), 117
Tours, *163*, *173*, *179*
Toveri (newspaper), 114
Trabucco, Chester, 131, 158, 184
Treaty of Ghent, 26, 188
Trolley, first electric, 85; downtown tour, 180; replacement by buses, 194, Riverfront, 154, *155*, 174, 180, 196
Trullinger Geer, Belle, 107
Trullinger, John C., 97, 192
Trullinger, Mrs. John C., 108
Union Fishermen's Cooperative Packing Company, *101*, 102, 174, 193
Union Fishermen's Net Drying Loft, *65*, 178
Union Packing Company, 68, 174
Uniontown, 68, 106, 114, 174, 192
Uniontown-Alameda Historic District, 174
United States Army Corps of Engineers, 63, 89

United States Bureau of Indian Affairs, 145
United States Coast Guard, early history, 52, 92, 190; modern-day 63, 144, 146-148, 158; operations 55, 118, *147*, 148, 177, 195, 196; war years, 138-139. *See also* lighthouse service, lightships, lighthouses
United States Federal Housing Administration (FHA), 136
United States Life Saving Service, 93, *93*, 146
United States Post Office, 36-37, 46, *47*, 59, 84, 180, 191
United States Quarantine Station (Knappton Cove), 97-98, *99*, 172, 193, 195. *See* "Ellis Island of the Columbia"
Upper Astoria (Uppertown), 42, 46, 48, 67-68, 78-80, 84-85, 88, *102-103*, 177, 193
Uppertown Firefighters Museum, 170
U. S. S. *Peacock* (naval ship), 10
U. S. S. *Shark* (naval ship), 189
Vancouver, George, 7, 187
Van Dusen, Adam, 58, 75, 189
Van Dusen, Willis, 58, 156
Victorian architectural-style homes, 1, 52, 160, *165-167*, 168, *169*, 170, 182, 184
War of 1812, 24, 26, 188
Washington/Oregon Columbia River Compact, 194
Weinhard-Astoria Hotel, *124*, 126, 170, *203*
Weinhard, Henry, 126
Welch, James, 36, 38, 85, 189, 190
West Mooring Basin, 102, 174
West, Oswald, 111
Wide West, The (ship), *76*, 78
Wilkes, Charles, 9-10, 29, 197
Willamette Falls and Paper Company, 96
William and Ann (ship), 28
Wilson, A. E., 21, 23, 35, 42, 117, 120, 188, 198
Wilson Shipbuilding Company, 117, 120
Women's Christian Temperance Union, 104, 106
Women's rights (suffrage), *107*, 106-108, 190, 194
Wood, Ben, 38
Works Progress Administration (WPA), 136
World War I, 114, 116, 120-121
World War II, 63, 71-72, 96, 117, 138-141, 158, 168, 186
Yakama tribe, 111, *112-113*
Young's Bay, 84, 94, 120, 136, 169, 192, 193
Young's River Falls (OR), 96, 166, 192

Courtesy Larry Kellis Photography.

Rivertide Publishing
www.rivertidepublishing.com